any diffrent.
- SM

CONTENTS

Ghost Stories &
Hippie Sh*t

KIMBERLY BIZJAK

The events and conversations in this book have been set down to the best of the author's ability, although some names and details have been changed to protect the privacy of individuals.

ONE

◆ ◆ ◆

Earth

The Brick

I sat cross-legged in the dark on the cold, dirty basement floor of what used to be Salem Massachusetts' first firehouse. My tour group that night was the usual mix of curious people looking for a genuine paranormal experience during the otherwise cheesy Halloween season. In attendance, I had a young couple from Tennessee, a pair of high school sweethearts and their teenage boys from the next town over, and a few groups of friends who had perhaps imbibed in one too many cocktails before the midnight tour.

After I greeted everyone, I got the group together in the center of the room. We formed a circle, some sitting on the floor with me, others deciding to stand.

In the middle of us all, I'd displayed various ghost hunting equipment: A KII meter and a Mel Meter for picking up Electromagnetic Field (otherwise known as EMF); an audio recorder in hopes of catching an Electronic Voice Phenomena (EVP); a flashlight that was twisted into an almost-on, barely-off position so that a spirit might tap on it to light up the room; a Spirit Box for hearing the deceased speak using white noise, and a few other various gadgets— dowsing rods and the like. I started in on my usual spiel about the history of the firehouse building and the spirits we'd come into contact with there. I explained how the equipment worked and how part of our experience that night (as it went every night) was for us to investigate any paranormal activity and attempt to debunk it. We'd use logic, curiosity, and all my equipment to get to the bottom of any experiences we might have together. Next, I reminded my tourists that just moments before descending the staircase, we'd all peeked inside the closed restaurant one floor above our heads. By the light of the corner streetlamp, we could see that every chair inside had been placed atop a table before sweeping and closing that afternoon.

I assured them that we were alone in the building. And, as far as I knew then and can claim now, we were.

"Is anyone upstairs?" I asked.

Silence.

"If there's anyone upstairs, can you drag a chair across the floor for me?"

We heard it directly overhead, the sound of metal slowly scraping against wood. All of my tourists gasped and held tightly to the person next to them.

"Thank you," I called out, happy we were off to an exciting start. Sometimes it took awhile for the activity to ramp up, and even though the build-up made the eventual experience payout sweeter, it was always a huge relief when the spirits came right out. Ghosts hold no guarantees, after all.

I'd heard the shrill scraping sound many times before. Not every night, but most nights. As I told every group I toured: not a single sound was staged. I did not have an employee sitting behind a counter upstairs waiting to tip-toe over to take a chair off of a table and slide it across the floor. I have no explanation for this paranormal phenomena, other than... it's paranormal. My job wasn't to create these experiences, it was simply to witness them and to hold the space for spirits and tourists alike.

I focused my attention on the ghost hunting equipment on the floor in front of me and said, "We're very excited to communicate with you tonight. Will you please come join us down here and move those lights on that KII meter from green to red?."

Silence.

"We'd all love to know that you're here tonight. Please light up the meter if you can."

One tiny flicker of red light appeared and just as quickly disappeared.

"Thank you," I said. "I have an audio recorder here. We might not be able to hear you, but if you speak very loudly into the recorder, we might be able to hear you when we listen back to the recording. Can you say your name as loudly as you can?"

Just then, in the pitch-black far corner of the basement, we heard a thunderous bang followed by what sounded like crumbling rocks hitting the floor, as if someone had thrown a brick into the darkness. One girl screamed out while the rest of the group audibly gasped. You could almost taste the adrenaline pulsing through the room. I definitely don't scare easily, but I was just as startled as my tourists, jumping alongside them, holding in my own gasp. In all the many tours I'd given in the firehouse, I'd never heard that sound before—but that night was different. I noticed that the energy shifted in that moment. I'd never experienced the feeling of negative energy in that space before. Prickly tingles crept down my neck and all along my spine. I couldn't let my fear show, though; I needed to be professional and also practice what I preached to this group earlier in the evening and attempt to debunk the noise before jumping to conclusions.

"Hmm, I've never heard that noise before," I said, "but this building *was* built in 1861. Surely bricks fall off the wall and crumble on occasion. Old buildings are always settling." With a deep breath I continued, "If that was you, could you use one of these pieces of equipment to let us know you're here instead?"

We sat in uncomfortable silence for a moment, though in the

clamminess of our collective panic it felt like several minutes. During a typical evening investigation, we hear a name at some point, or perhaps we'd hear another word or light tapping noise. Sometimes the flashlight would turn on and off on command, sometimes the temperature would drop.

That night, as I said before, was quite different.

The Tennessean man yelled, "Kim! I think I see a shadow in that corner!"

Everyone turned immediately and clung to the person next to them, stranger or not. Arms were linked, breathing was getting heavier, and the space was feeling somehow larger and darker by the moment.

I'd noticed the shadow too. It looked like a dark almost-human shape that appeared near the ceiling and slid down the wall to the floor in a heap. Nothing like that had ever happened on my tours— or even in my own, personal adventures— before.

At that point, I was ready to start packing up and turn on the lights, and end my tour a bit early. I switched on the red light of the Mel Meter and pointed it at the corner where the shadow had been. Nothing was there. Relieved, I pointed the light to the other three corners of the room, and breathed a little easier when I found nothing unusual.

Paranormal is one thing... brick-wielding shadow creatures are another.

"Can we turn the lights on in here now?" The question came from the same terrified girl who'd let out the scream just a few minutes before.

"Sure, we can finish the tour in the lobby of the offices on the upper floors if you'd all like."

There were nods. Everyone agreed to pack the equipment and get out of there as fast as possible.

After loading my ghost hunting equipment into a bag I carried over one shoulder, I held the Mel Meter with it's red glowing flashlight in my other hand and shined it on the floor to lead us toward the exit. We walked slowly, huddled together, making our way toward the door, staying as far against the opposite wall from that shadowy corner as we could. I was about to illuminate that corner again when a single red brick flew through the air, headed right for our heads, straight from the nothingness of the dark. We ducked, hands covering ourselves as best we could. I fumbled with my equipment but managed to get out of the way. The brick smashed into the wall behind the group, showering us with rocky debris.

We didn't run. We didn't breathe. We were frozen.

After the long beat between the dust settling around us and our adrenals firing up again, we started pushing each other forward.

"Go, go, go!" I wasn't alone in shouting this direction. We'd started out as a regular group of tourists and tour guide. But now we were comrades, escaping a quickly escalating, unsafe situation. Up until that night, in all my experiences over the years, ghosts had never really acted out. They weren't typically malicious— maybe they were bitter or didn't want us there, but they'd never attempted to harm anyone.

This, however, didn't seem like the average ghost.

I led them all up the tall, winding stairwell and into the updated modern office spaces two floors up and turned on the lights. We walked down the hallway and into the main lobby filled with fluorescent lights and collapsed onto comfortable chairs and couches, breathing heavily. It was such a stark contrast to what we knew was just a staircase away.

"What was that?!" Someone asked, incredulous. Several of them echoed the same question, some immediately retelling their own experiences, comparing it to one another.

I listened to them share their stories, building their collective narrative, but mostly, I was thinking about how my liability insurance very likely *did not* cover guests injured by paranormal entities with ill intentions. How could I play this cool and keep myself safe from any legal repercussions?

Sure, I talk to ghosts for a living... But that's the thing: this was my business. And as far as I know, none of the spirits I've worked with have been lawyers with enough experience to get me out of being sued for ghostly negligence.

I interjected, "I'm not sure what happened down there, but there has to be a logical explanation." Everyone quieted down. "Let's listen back to the audio and see if we caught anything."

I announced it just as quickly as I thought to do it.

The bag over my shoulder swung down with a shrug and I rummaged through until I found my audio recorder. I plugged a small speaker into it and pressed play. My voice echoed back to me: "I have an audio recorder here. We might not be able to hear you, but if you speak very loudly into the recorder, we might be able to hear you when we listen back to the recording. Can you say your name as loudly as you can?"

Silence.

And then... "GO! HOME!" I pushed stop on the recorder and replayed it. "GO! HOME!" It was as clear as my own voice. Deep and bellowing, he sounded angry.

My group was speechless. They didn't gasp this time; I don't think they were breathing.

Several thoughts flooded my head as I replayed his voice a few more times. One piece of working with intuition is processing a lot of information very quickly. I have heard quite the variety of different voices on my audio recorder during my many nights of ghost hunting, and I've even heard disembodied voices saying, "go home" before. This voice was different however. It made me feel scared, yet sad at the same time. I considered my fear, my group's fear, *his* fear. What did we do to make this man so upset? Who was he? Why is he in the basement? What did he need to help him cross over?

I thought of how lonely it must be to be stuck in a basement for all of eternity, with only tourist groups to keep you company. And even then, we were just disturbing the only place he could call home, this lost soul. Shadow creature or not, he was as real as any of the people in the basement that night, and I knew I had to help. What else were my abilities for?

These thoughts hadn't crossed my mind until that night. When I started Paranormal Salem, it was because I saw a desire for it and I thought I could make good money at it. I loved paranormal stuff! Watching ghost shows on television thrilled me, and after training with TAPS Academy in Rhode Island, I began offering tourists the chance to experience the paranormal in a unique way that hadn't been done before. I never once thought of the spirits. Why are they here? How can I help them? Who are they? Are they accused witches from 1692 or are they family members of one of my tourists and they desperately need to get a message across to them? That night I felt there was a much greater force leading me to ponder these questions.

I didn't end up here, with this particular set of skills and interests, by accident.

So what led me here?

I've always believed that I had a perfectly normal upbringing. I wasn't born into a family of witches or mystical crystal-ball-gazing card readers. I don't have a cat-lady aunt who always claimed to have some claim to a lineage of psychic women. I've never had a near-death experience. I've never seen a ghoulish figure standing at the foot of my bed.

But when I think back on the journey to becoming who I am today, I realize that maybe my upbringing wasn't very "normal," at all, at least by most standards.

What's "normal," anyway?

Childhood Imagination

I believe telling our tales of paranormal experiences from our youth helps to normalize these unique moments that are surprisingly common. Children and young adults are much more attuned to things outside our usual realm of existence. I think that perhaps it's because they have yet to learn what they're expected to see, and instead truly seek out their own perspective. Every moment of their young lives is completely fresh! As we get older, we assimilate more and more into the reality we've created alongside other adults—the one we've all agreed upon— and witnessing these anomalies can become more challenging. In this chapter, you'll learn about some of the early life experiences I had as a young medium who knew nothing of what was to come in her unusually magical life.

Like so many other children who grow up sequestered in the soggy forests of the Pacific Northwest, I spent a great deal of my young girlhood adventuring in the company of the flora, fauna, and an imaginary friend. Many children have imaginary friends and such presences are often brushed off by family members as creative coping mechanisms, but I'm not entirely sure what to make of my own imaginary friend experience. Rather curiously, I don't remember anything about him. My parents have told me stories about how I would talk about him constantly, what we'd do together, and how involved he was in my life. Here's what I know from their retellings:

I always insisted on leaving a chair at the dinner table open for my playmate, and I always made sure to invite him to sit on the empty swing next to me at the playground. In my mind, he was a part of our family. My parents used to reminisce and laugh about his name: A.B. "What kind of name is A.B.?", they wondered aloud with smiles. "That isn't a name, just letters." Maybe they were the only two letters that I knew as a toddler? Thinking back now, maybe A.B. wasn't a figment of my imagination after all; maybe he was a spirit. Maybe I was practicing my mediumship abilities at an early age without realizing it. When I see clients today for readings I usually hear the general sound and syllables of a name but not quite the whole name. Sometimes I only understand the first couple letters and I have to piece the rest together. Maybe A.B. were initials, or maybe his name was Abe? Abey? Or even Abby, and perhaps he was actually a she? I suppose I'll never know. I'm not sure what happened to my maybe-ghostly friend. I'm not sure if I just stopped talking about him— or her, or them— one day, or if my parents became annoyed or embarrassed and told me to stop. Or perhaps A.B. left, crossed over, or simply moved on to another lonely child. I really don't know. Wherever they are, I just hope they're at peace.

Some things, however, I do remember. My elementary school days were, overall, unremarkably average. Our neighborhood was always swirling with kids and I spent most of my time playing outdoors with my friends. Caterpillars and slugs and stray cats became friends we played with until we returned them to the wilds they came from, and we returned to games of superheroes and house and other distractions of our own design. We climbed trees and caught tadpoles and frogs in the muddy pond behind my house. Beyond the pond was a greenbelt of evergreen trees that the neighborhood kids referred to as simply "the woods." No one went into the woods alone; it felt creepy, all dark, wet, and full of moss, plus... there were stories about ghosts and monsters in there. I'm not sure why I always wanted to spend time there. I never experienced anything paranormal in those woods, but I think I liked the thrill of it.

After spending a day in the woods, I would feel terrified when I went to bed at night. My imagination would run wild. I could swear that I sensed a presence under my bed, and I could hear knocking noises coming from my closet. I would stand up on my bed and jump as far as I could, as fast as I could, over to the light switch. I wonder now what causes the common "monster under the bed" fear in children. I always assumed it was over-active imagination, but who knows?

Sleepovers And
Ouija Boards

I n my middle school years, I'm not sure when or why, but I started to practice what I now know to be called automatic writing. I'd sit in my room and write questions on a piece of notebook paper, then hold the pencil in my hand with the tip to the paper, eyes closed, breathing deeply, waiting for my pencil to move. Sometimes, thoughts that I knew were not my own would come into my mind and I'd somewhat consciously write them down. Other times, my pencil would scribble furiously, then stop, and I'd open my eyes to find answers scrawled out as if by magic. What struck me the most the first few times this happened— and it still does surprise me on occasion— was that I had no awareness of the words that had been written whatsoever. Each answer was always a surprise!

I would write back and forth like this to a ghost friend for years. He told me his name was Yeley. Again, just as with my imaginary friend A.B., I wonder: what kind of name is Yeley? Is that a last name? Did I get letters mixed up somehow? Was I only picking up the rough sound of the name? I would talk to this spirit during my early teenage years in my diary and ask advice. Typical young girl questions like, "Does this boy like me? Am I ugly?" I believed I was receiving guidance from a very wise friend who was not of this world.

And maybe I was. Maybe he was my angel helping me through all those iconically awkward early teenage years.

While continuing to do my automatic writing, I became very interested in all things "psychic." I'd check out books from the library on ways to form and strengthen one's psychic senses, and then do the exercises in my journal alongside my conversations with Yeley.

On one trip to the library, I found a hypnotism video designed to help the viewer access their sixth sense. I checked it out and brought it to a sleepover. When my friend and I were certain her parents had gone to sleep, we turned on the cheesy video of swirling blue lights, a monotone male voice telling us that all we had to do to become psychic was to close our eyes and in your mind think the words, "Sixth Sense." We were instructed by the faceless guide to practice by having a friend or family member think of a shape inside their head, and by thinking the words "Sixth Sense," we would be able to tell them what shape they were imagining.

We tried it the next school day.

To my surprise, it worked. It really worked. Our friends would think of a shape, and we would tell them what they were thinking. I'd close my eyes, think "Sixth Sense," and I'd see a shape in my mind's eye. Square! Circle! Rectangle! Star! My success rate far surpassed my friend's, which didn't seem to bother her much since it was still a cool thing we were doing together— as any grown woman will tell you, young girls and supernatural phenomena go together like fish and water. It was like a party trick that our friends couldn't figure out. Other than my one friend's approval and excitement, though, my reputation for being "weird" was beginning to precede me, and my classmates were a bit freaked out.

I stopped being so open about my abilities once I realized I was feeling more and more estranged from my peers. Instead of a friend, I felt like they viewed me as some strange outsider— at the very least they saw me as the quirky, odd person out, but possibly the worst thing I felt them projecting onto me was that I was lying about who I was and what I could do. In addition to all the ostracization and isolation, I was also called names. "Crazy" was the most popular.

Hiding myself just seemed like an easier option.

Other people choosing to do occult-related activities, however, received a free pass from my suppression. After all, if I wasn't the one suggesting the "weird" stuff, I couldn't be judged nearly so harshly.

One day in the locker room after gym class, when a girl took a ouija board out of her locker, I was naturally fascinated. Everyone, including me, gasped, scandalized.

"Oh come on! Let's play with it!" she said.

I'd never seen a ouija board in person and I was super curious. Only four of us stayed behind while the rest of the students quickly headed off to the cafeteria for lunch.

We put the board on one of the benches between our lockers and kneeled on the floor around it. Gently, each of us placed our fingertips on the planchette.

"What is your name?" the owner of the ouija board asked. I didn't dare provoke more rumors, so I stayed quiet, there for the ride more than anything.

The planchette moved in circles hitting random letters that didn't make any sense.

"You're moving it," one girl said to the group.

"I'm not! Are you moving it?" said another.

"Okay, let's try asking it a yes or no question first," the leader of our little seance suggested. "Are you a boy?"

The planchette moved to *Yes.*

"How did you die?"

The planchette started moving slowly this time, not in circles but with what seemed like purpose.

H...O...W...D...I...D...Y...O...U...D...I...E

Gasps and squeals swirled through our foursome. "The board is asking how *we* died!?"

We put the board back in the box and left the empty locker room in a rush, giggling and retelling details of our story to one another in whispers.

The next time we had gym class, we thought we'd try again. We set it up on the bench again and began asking questions, picking up exactly where we'd left off.

"We are *not* dead. Do you know that you are dead?"

The planchette moved to *No.*

Then started moving slowly toward the letters again.

K...U...R...T...C...O...B...A...I...N

"Kurt Cobain?!" I exclaimed, "You guys are stupid! You're moving it! Stop it!"

We all ran off to lunch, much less enthralled than the first time, and didn't bring out the ouija board again.

Roughly two weeks later, I sat in my science class when my seatmate ran into class in tears.

"Did you guys hear?!" she sobbed to the class, "Kurt Cobain died!"

Like my classmates, I sat there stunned with my mouth wide open. Unlike my classmates, my shock wasn't because Nirvana was my favorite band, nor was I in the throes of teenage love with the late singer.   I wasn't mourning like this girl next to me— I was reflecting that a ouija board had quite possibly predicted the tragically young death of one of the most iconic musicians in the world.

◆ ◆ ◆

Another night in middle school, a friend had me come to a sleepover at her house. We were sitting on top of our sleeping bags on the floor of her room eating our weight in potato chips, a parade of candy wrappers surrounding our criss-crossed legs. By the dim light of her single bedside lamp, I began to tell her the scariest story I could think of between bites of SweeTarts. It was a classic tale of teenage horror, one I think I must have amalgamated from several myths, legends, and folklore I'd amassed throughout my adolescence.

After a long afternoon of playing games and making dinner, a young babysitter put the boy she's watching overnight to bed upstairs and collapsed on the living room couch to watch TV. When she flicks on the television, the news anchor onscreen announced a deranged patient had escaped from the insane asylum a few towns over, and told viewers to remain inside. "Lock those doors, ladies and gentlemen," the news anchor said in a dramatic voice, before handing over the scene to the weather man. She was freaked out, so she got up and flipped on every light in the house. She locked the front door, checked all the windows, and slid the deadbolt into place on the back door. Feeling a bit better, she curled up on the couch and switched the channel to some laugh-track sitcom. She fell asleep watching.

A few hours later, she woke to the sound of infomercials and a repetitive squeaking noise coming from upstairs. Creeeeak, creeeeak, creeeeak. She climbed the stairs to the rec room. In the dark, she could barely make out the shape of a woman sitting in a rocking chair, rocking back and forth, back and forth. The woman was facing the wall, head bobbing slowly, forward and back. Terrified, the babysit-

ter grabbed a toy bat and walked over to the intruder as quietly as she could. Her whole body shook. As she got closer, she could see the woman's emotionless eyes staring straight ahead at the wall as she rocked back and forth, back and forth.

That's when the babysitter, trembling, let out a blood-curdling scream as she looked down at the woman's lap and saw the little boy's bloody head, and the woman's long, withered fingers pulling out the hairs on his head one

by

one.

I pretended to pluck a hair from my friend's head for dramatic effect.

"Okay!" she shrieked, half-laughing as she startled, "I'm done! No more stories! I'm gonna have nightmares."

I giggled and we unwrapped more candy.

That's when the light bulb on the lamp on her table suddenly flickered off and the whole room went pitch black.

We screamed and both jumped up and ran for the light switch. The light overhead turned on before turning back off. Dark again. Frightened and frantic, we opened the door to the hallway and ran out. She turned the lights on and, thankfully, this time they didn't go out. My friend's mom opened her bedroom door and asked us with a yawn what in the world we were screaming about at two in the morning. We tripped over each other's words, manically recounting the scary story and the sequence of events, but she just told us we were scaring ourselves and that there was nothing to be afraid of. "Go to bed, girls." We didn't even need to consult one another about the fact that neither of us was going back into her bedroom. Instead, we went to the living room to watch TV and get our minds off of what had just happened. A few minutes in, the volume started increasing and decreasing on its own, crackling loudly out of the speakers and then quieting down to a barely-audible murmur. Still freaked out, she fiddled with the remote, turning the television off and back on. It seemed to function normally after that. We fell asleep to the sounds of laugh tracks, just like the ill-fated protagonist of my story just minutes earlier.

I don't think we really slept much that night.

The next morning, on the ride to my house, her parents' car radio started switching channels without any of us touching the dial. Her mom scoffed at the songs that came through— not her taste, after all— and tinkered with the controls while we sat screaming in the back seat.

"Calm down, girls," she sighed, "no need to get worked up over a faulty radio."

It seemed that all of my friend's family's electronics were a bit wonky after that for quite a while.

Black Hair Dye And Horror Movies

During the notoriously rebellious years of high school, I explored— and perhaps trampled all over— the limits of both fashion and social norms via black hair dye and horror movies. My favorite was Scream. It had so many references to classic horror movies that my friends and I were inspired to go back and start at the beginning— we'd rent every horror movie they had. Classics like Halloween, Friday the 13th, and Nightmare on Elm Street. And weird one-off cheesy ones, like the one about the demented dentist with a penchant for collecting teeth. This was all back in the days of Blockbuster, when you'd walk through a video store to choose which movie you wanted to watch that evening rather than browse the latest releases on media streaming services. Part of the process that I loved so much was the entire ritual of visiting the video store, examining the cardboard and plastic movie covers, carefully choosing the title we'd be watching that night. I was obsessed. My friend and I even started writing our own horror movie script for a potential film that we cleverly titled *Scream 2 ½.* At school, we'd constantly regale our classmates (and each other) about the plot of the movie, asking our friends if they'd play various victims, and describing various theatrical ways to kill someone. Sometimes, someone would enthusiastically volunteer to act as the casualty of a particularly entertaining murder. Things changed, however, after the tragic Columbine school shooting. Thinking of that horrific event, scary movies became less... fun after that. We never finished our script and to this day, I'm not a horror fan. Real life— and death— is horror enough for my taste.

Thinking about death in a real way can be terrifying. I would constantly ponder the universe, our existence, and what happened when we died. At nighttime, I would lay awake in my bed, so scared, thinking, "Some day I am going to die. Me. It's going to happen and there's nothing I can do about it." I'd worry about my family and my friends too, writing pages and pages in my journal of questions I had about our existence.

Here is one such journal entry written by my teenage self:

"Have you ever noticed how your hands look underwater? They look like someone else's hands. Someone you've never seen or met. Have you ever said a word so many times in a row that it begins to sound like you've never heard or said it before? Have you ever sat and listened to the dial tone of a telephone? After a while it begins to change and sound different. Have you ever passed by something every day and finally decide to stop and look at it? It looks like you've never seen it before. It looks new. Have you ever looked at the sky for so long that it begins to change colors? White, dark blue, blue-green, maybe even some sparkles that make it look fuzzy? Have you ever noticed there's a thin black lining on everything you look at? Does black only line non-living things? Do living things have a colored lining? An aura?

What's deja vu? Does your body just react a certain way to make you think you've been there and done that before? Or have you really done that? Maybe in a past life? Do you believe in reincarnation? Do you believe in heaven and hell? Which would you prefer? Is heaven a warm, peaceful place? Is hell hot with burning flames? Or is it cold, very cold and empty? Maybe hell is your worst fear on earth. Is the torture different for each person? Is heaven different for each person? Most people think of heaven as a sunny place where you walk on clouds and listen to gospel music. What if you like rain and rock music? Is it a good thing to be in heaven forever? Would you get bored? Reincarnation sounds much more fun.

Have you ever thought that there might just be one unavoidable thing on Earth that causes you to die? Maybe if you never, in your whole life, smelled a flower or been hit with a leaf falling from a tree, that you'd live forever? Does growing up hurt? Does life hurt more than dying? Is death painful? Are you scared of dying? Are you afraid of the possible pain or what will come of you after? Dead. That's all. Six feet underground. Maybe it's just an endless dreamless sleep? Does believing in the afterlife depend on your religion? How did so many religions get started? Do you pray? Why do you pray with your head down when heaven is supposedly up? Do you believe in God? What if God was just made up for your enjoyment or something to fall back on? It's just like Santa and the Easter Bunny. Did you cry when you found out they were only imaginary? (It's not that I don't believe in God, I'm just not sure I trust the people who say they work for him.) Saying there is, in fact, a God, is God male or female? Is God only one person? Is God even a person? Where did God come from? Did God have parents? Maybe the role of God gets passed down to others like a king or a president. Maybe there's multiple gods like the Greek and Roman beliefs? Does one god run it all, or is there one God for each planet with life?

Do you believe there is life out there in the universe other than us? Why do people of Earth think aliens look green with slimy ooze dripping from their tubes and tentacles? Why can't other life forms look like humans? Would they speak one of our many languages on Earth? Maybe all of them? Humans share the Earth with other species, like animals and insects. Do other planets have multiple species like we do? Would aliens be more or less intelligent than us? Would they be ahead of us with their technology? Would they know the answers to all these questions that we can't answer?

Where did we come from? Where did the universe come from? Scientists believe in the 'Big Bang Theory'. They think that is what created planets. But a big bang from what? A big sun? Where did the big sun come from? Where did space come from? Air, just space. How or where does space end? A brick wall? What's the other side of the brick wall? More space! It never ends! Maybe it's one big circle. You travel so far in the universe you eventually end up where you started? Is that why comets eventually come back to earth? Does it really have to do with orbit and gravity? When a comet swings by earth and then eventually swings by again thousands of years later, how do scientists know it's the same comet?

I want to be a comet, or maybe just hitch a ride. I'd travel for thousands of years. Maybe I'll meet some aliens and they'd invite me in for tea, or some green alien ooze. Eventually I'd swing back around to Earth someday and tell Earth people of my travels and all I have seen. I'll tell them that when I went so far through space I noticed that stars are only holes punched into a huge piece of black construction paper."

MOHAI

In the late 90's, I was working on the event staff at the Museum of History and Industry (MOHAI) in Seattle, Washington. One night in particular, there was a wedding reception in the 1880's-themed room, and all evening long, we ran into problems with the sound system. It would turn off without warning, seemingly for no reason, which— if you don't already know— doesn't really work for weddings, or for the venues those parties are paying to provide a seamless experience.

It was always creepy in that museum when you were the last ones there late at night. This was all well before my ghost hunter training and mediumship had taken off, so though I know *now* that ghosts aren't inherently scary, I had no idea what to expect in the dark of the night back then. Despite my own training and the firsthand knowledge that ghosts *really* truly aren't scary, I still got nervous during the closing shift.

The reception ended and eventually all of the party-goers were gone. It was just my co-worker Sarah and I there left to clean up, fold up all the tables, and put away the sound equipment.

Everyone on staff knew the museum was haunted by an elderly woman who once worked as a librarian there. She had a habit of screwing around with the sound system. As far as hauntings go, this one was definitely on the harmless side, but it could get rather tedious at times, especially when there was so much else to do. By the third malfunction I joked to my coworker, "Just ask the nice librarian if she would please leave the speakers alone for the evening." As if by miracle, we didn't run into another issue all night long. I quietly thanked the librarian.

I carried two chairs under each arm around the corner to store behind an exhibit of an 1880's storefront. As I passed the emergency exit door, I heard a distinct *knock knock*.

I figured someone must have forgotten their bag or jacket.

Usually the emergency exits are armed with alarm systems, but this night in particular they were shut off for the event, so I set the chairs against the wall and pulled the handle, swinging the door open. Nobody was there, only darkness. I shrugged and assumed it was the wind knocking something against the door, or maybe the sound came from somewhere else. Like just about anyone else would have, my brain instantly rationalized what had happened. I picked up the chairs, slid them behind the exhibit, and started walking back toward the main hall. Out of nowhere, loud footsteps thundered past me, rushing down the hallway. I couldn't see anyone with me. My breathing stopped. Adrenaline coursed through my body, my heart hammered away in my chest, and I felt electric. My face flushed and the energy in the room changed; You know that feeling you get when your foot falls asleep? The entire room felt like that. Static. Charged. Uncomfortable.

I yelled Sarah's name.
"What?" She replied from around the corner.
"Did you hear that?" I asked.
"Hear what?"
"Knocking sounds? Footsteps?" I asked, a little more frantic than I'd like to admit.
"Okay stop freaking me out."

"I'm freaking out. You might as well freak out with me. There was a knock at the door and no one was there. And then it sounded like footsteps ran past me! You didn't hear anything at all?"

The room kept buzzing. We kept working, putting everything away and sweeping the floors, but we picked up the pace, trying to get out of there as soon as we could. It just felt *wrong* to be there. We were on opposite ends of the room when I heard Sarah gasp.

"I swear I just heard someone say my name behind me!" she said.

Again, adrenaline flooded me like lava. "Okay, stop it!" I yelled, maybe at whatever entity had joined us that night, maybe at Sarah. "Let's just hurry up and get out of here. The floors look fine."

Each exhibit had its own breaker box, hidden away strategically within the displays, and each box contained a series of switches connected to various lights throughout the entire museum.

"Okay, you turn the lights off in the right wing, I'll turn them off in the left wing, and I'll meet you at the top of the stairs." I said, obviously forgetting the first rule of any scary movie: never split up.

I lifted a hidden panel in the storefront façade and switched the breakers off with a clunk. The lights in that exhibit went dark and I quickly moved to the next room. I walked behind a Native American display, found the next breaker box, and with another series of *clunk-clunk-clunks*, I sent the carefully positioned mannequins into darkness.

Now remember, this was before everyone had a smartphone with a flashlight. Mannequins, in the dark of a closed, quiet museum at night? Just as goosebump-inducing as one might think.

Working my way through the left wing I felt a lot of unease, constantly checking behind to make sure nothing out of the ordinary was happening. I made it through the wing without any strange occurrences or noises and walked, relieved, to the top of the stairs to meet Sarah. Double checking behind us that all the lights were off and only the stairwell was lit, we continued down the stairs to close up the lower floor of the museum.

"I'm not going in that storage room. You do it," Sarah said. One of us had to.

Old buildings are weird for a lot of reasons. This one in particular had some electrical quirks due to the layout. The entire downstairs of the museum was on one breaker box that was located all the way at the end of a sprawling labyrinth of storage. At closing time, this room— where all the museum's random donated items and other equipment were stored—was without lights because we'd already switched off the breaker upstairs. We still had to switch off the *other* breakers that were in this room, though. This extremely unpleasant, strange room. Floor to ceiling chain link fencing encapsulated the long stretch of corridor that led to the breaker box.

"You are going to make me go in there by myself? No way. You're coming with me," I demanded.

As soon as we opened the door to the room, I grabbed the flashlight that staff kept sitting on a chair just inside the door; no one liked the storage room in the dark, but this night in particular felt extra *nope*-worthy.

"Can't I just watch you from here?" Sarah pleaded.

On second thought, it wasn't such a bad idea. "Actually, yes. Stand here and hold the door open so more light shines in."

I started walking down the hallway, trying not to peek in at all of the creepy items that were stored on either side of me. Mannequins, old furniture, even the stuffed carcass of a real gorilla, its teeth gleaming in the white glare of the flashlight. I looked ahead, narrowing my focus. When I finally reached the breaker box, the sound of breathing crept up, right behind my ears. I swung around expecting to see Sarah behind me, but she was still standing on the far end holding the door open.

I don't think I've ever run so fast in my life.

"Someone was breathing in my ear. Let's go!"

Sarah's face went just as pale as mine. She knew just as well as I did that the museum really wasn't a place anyone wanted to be at night.

We closed the door as I was still trying to catch my breath. I wasn't sure I wanted to keep working at the museum.

"Okay, let's put the sound equipment away and get out of here," Sarah said. She waggled the microphones in her hand at me, and I remembered the cables I had draped over my shoulders. We weren't out of the dark just yet.

While we walked to the theatre lobby, Sarah said, "Why don't you go through the house doors and put those microphones away in the booth, and I'll walk through this backstage door and put these cables away in the cabinet."

I agreed (Again, why did we keep deciding to split up?) and walked a few doors down from her. As I was fiddling with my keys, trying to find the correct one, I heard her from inside say, "Hi!" I opened my door and saw her standing on the stage. She screamed.

"What?!" I screamed back.

"I just saw a shadow in the dark, I assumed it was you, walking from that door to the booth... Then you opened the door."

"Okay, I cannot believe all of the terrifying things that have happened tonight. No one is going to believe us," I said as I switched on every light in the theatre.

I ran to the booth, put the microphones in their bin, and ran back out. She jumped off the stage and joined me at the auditorium doors. We reluctantly turned off the lights in the theatre that we had just turned on, and the rest of the lights in the lower floor of the building, set the alarm, and went outside into the dreary, far less exciting, standard rainy Seattle night. I'd parked very close to our exit and Sarah was parked at the front of the building. I offered to give her a ride around to her car. As I drove past the front entrance of the museum, we gasped as we saw that every light that we had turned off that night was back on.

We completely lost our cool at that point (as if we had any cool left). After we settled down, we decided to call our boss despite the late hour; We didn't want to be penalized for closing the museum improperly.

"Hello, Michelle? It's Kim and Sarah.
"What's up, you guys?"
"I know you're going to think we're *completely* crazy and you won't believe this, but... we just finished turning off every breaker and alarmed the building, and then we drove around to the front of the building... Every single light is back on."
"Oh," she said in the most nonchalant possible tone, "that's ok. It's just the ghost. Don't worry about it. Have a good night!"

College Theatre, And Ghost Hunting

In 2004, I began attending Cornish College of the Arts to earn my Bachelor of Fine Arts in Performance Production (Sound Design) for Theatre.

Why are theatres always considered haunted? I've spent a lot of my time in many different theatres, and I believe the experiences people have tend to be related to the sheer number of audience members who come for a show, and the energy they leave circulating behind. There's also a *huge* amount of energy exchanged between the actors and the crowd, because performances are meant to invoke deep feelings and emotions. It might also have to do with the furniture, props, and costumes. Most is donated and could possibly carry the energy of their deceased previous owner, or even the energy of the actor who used or wore the item last, or most passionately.

Shadow figures are something I've encountered in several different theatres. Sometimes near the audience seats, sometimes on stage, sometimes in the catwalk (the passageway above the stage where the lights are suspended) or up in the sound booth. This happened in my high school performing arts center, and also in the Reisbeck Performance Hall at Cornish quite frequently. One of my classes was a private, one-on-one

Sound Design class which took place in a room that was only accessible through a door on the far end of the sound booth. The stairs to the booth rose right next to a row of windows with dark curtains. On days I had class, I would enter the darkened auditorium alone and hurriedly shuffle to the stairs of the booth, walking up them while avoiding looking at the pitch-black theatre space to my left. Upon reaching the door to the booth, I'd type in the access code as fast as I could, closing the door tight behind me. One day as I was heading up the stairs to class, I raced up the first four steps when the curtain billowed against my foot as a disembodied voice bellowed *"raarr!"*

I kept running up the stairs and arrived in class trying not to look as terrified as I felt; there was no use sharing my creepy story and adding more fuel to the "crazy" fire.

A few days later, the theatre was lit and filled with other classmates, so I decided to see if the windows had the ability to open at all. I thought that, maybe, there had been someone standing outside that day trying to scare me.

But those windows were sealed shut.

When I was the assistant sound designer for a show at the Seattle Repertory Theatre, I noticed shadows and noises there, too. Honestly, any theatre I have been in all have a very distinct *creepy* feeling. During a tour of the Moore Theatre in Seattle, I noticed the side balconies had a similar energy to them. However, Ghost Hunters had filmed an episode there, and during their investigation they found that there was a very high EMF reading in those areas... due to old wiring. Some things have totally bland, easily-digested explanations. Others don't. Perhaps this is why I've always loved paranormal and supernatural television shows.

I used to be a big fan of *Crossing Over with John Edward*. I was awestruck by how he would read strangers with such accuracy.

Still, I was always a bit skeptical. How does he do that? How could he possibly know this information? Where does it come from? While I was fascinated by his incredible readings, his show left me with more questions than answers.

When *Ghost Hunters* first aired, I was hooked. This was something I could understand. They were using scientific equipment that *proved* the existence of ghosts. I could wrap my logical left brain around this concept and quickly became transfixed. I never missed a single episode. Still, I thought, it could all be a big hoax. Those EMF detectors *could* be rigged. I wanted to try ghost hunting for myself! Badly. But where does someone even start with that kind of thing?

◆ ◆ ◆

Then, I heard about a small museum in Capitol Hill in Seattle called The Museum of Mysteries that offered a "Haunted Lock-In" and a ghost hunting trip to the Harvard Exit Theatre.

I called my sister and asked if she wanted to join me.

Our tour began with six other people in a very small old room of the museum. It was filled with bookshelves and curios, occult paraphernalia related to unexplained phenomena— UFO's, Bigfoot, haunted houses, that kind of thing. Our guide told us ghost stories surrounding Capitol Hill and neighborhood businesses, the building that we were in, and Harvard Exit. They provided two KII meters for the group to share. An avid Ghost Hunters fan, I knew this piece of equipment pretty well in theory, but I listened intently as our guide told us the spiel— that EMF stood for Electromagnetic Field, and that spirits could use or change the EMF in the room to communicate with us. KII meters are typically used by electricians to check electrical boxes, and they aren't designed to stay in the "on" position. So, just like on Ghost Hunters, there was a penny wedged in the button so that it wouldn't turn off until you took it out. There was a series of lights on the meter. The first light was green and indicated that the meter was on and ready, and the last light was red. I was so excited to actually see a KII meter in person after watching them being used on TV each week. I couldn't wait until it was my turn to use it. We walked next door through the rain and made our way to the Harvard Exit.

Our tour guide told us that in the 1920's, the Harvard Exit was the home of the Women's Century Club, a group dedicated to women's rights. We heard stories about the apparition of a woman in 1920's clothing that was constantly seen floating in the room and on the stairs. Finally, we got to walk around with our KII meter to see if there were any "spikes"— the lights on the meter lighting all the way to red. When it was my turn to use it, I was just so excited that I didn't really spend any time investigating. Instead, I spent more time taking photos of my sister and myself inside the theatre, smiling with our KII meter in hand.

We walked through the building all the way to a small room at the back, while our guide told us stories about the strange EMF hits they often found there, and more details about the ghosts that haunted the museum. He said many guests claimed to hear voices or see shadows in the restroom, and that sometimes the restroom would be locked from the inside when no one was in there. When we asked to go check it out, our guide told us we all had to go in, together, to investigate. Creepy, right? Well, he didn't join us, which only added to the feeling of excited discomfort.

The restroom was a big open room with only one toilet, so there was plenty of space for us to gather around and stand up against the walls. As strange as it was to sit in a restroom in complete darkness with six other strangers, I finally felt like a real paranormal investigator, and I liked it. The only light visible in the room was the green light on each KII meter. I jumped right in to lead us on our investigation. With thoughts of Moaning Myrtle on my mind, I set one of the KII meters on the floor in front of us and another man did the same with his.

"Is there anyone in here with us?" I asked. "If you're here, could you please light up that meter?"

I swear the energy in the room changed... but the meter remained unchanged. A few people asked another question or two, then we all decided it was dumb to sit in a bathroom talking to nobody.

When we arrived back in the main room, we were directed toward a table set up with playing cards. Our tour guide told us that we were going to play a game of poker with their resident ghost, Peter Alexander. The museum property used to be the location of Washington's first legal post-prohibition Public House, and before that, it was most likely a speakeasy. He told us that Peter Alexander was a gambler and loved to interact with the EMF detector while playing cards with visitors.

So we each took a seat around the table, leaving one space open for Peter. Our guide dealt cards to each of us, leaving cards and a shot of whiskey at the empty seat face-down next to one of the KII meters. He told us to not show anyone our cards and use the chips to play a mock game of poker. We went through the motions, throwing chips in the middle and laughing nervously. When it was Peter's turn, the KII meter blinked from green to orange.

"No way!" Someone yelled. "That has to be rigged!"

We were assured that it was most definitely not rigged and that this happens all the time. We continued to play and when it was Peter's turn again, this time the light stayed on green.

"Maybe he doesn't like his cards this round," someone joked.

We played for about half an hour, and sometimes the KII meter would flash, sometimes it wouldn't. Did the evening convince me that Ghost Hunters and using scientific equipment was the real deal? Maybe.

I wanted my own equipment to find out.

TWO

◆ ◆ ◆

Fire

Salem, Massachusetts

I moved to Salem, Massachusetts with my husband and three-year-old son so that I could attend graduate school at Emerson College in Boston in 2009. We chose Salem because my husband's job was in the neighboring city of Danvers, and there was a commuter rail station that gave me easy access into Downtown Boston. But the main reason I wanted to move there? Halloween!

Halloween has *always* been my absolute favorite holiday. My husband and I have made a habit of throwing the best Halloween parties, hosting around 100 people each year. The costumes people have worn to these events are routinely nothing short of amazing. I take a lot of pride in my Halloween decorating skills — we've never been a store-bought plastic skeleton or window cling kind of house. Us? We stain sheets with tea and use them to cover all our furniture. We painstakingly hang cobwebs in every nook and cranny of the place. Each year, I bring out beautiful antique candelabras and disguise all our artwork with haunted art printed from the internet. One year, we had new carpet being installed two days after our party so, naturally, we covered the entire house with fake blood.

With all the years of ghoulish merriment I enjoyed on the west coast, I couldn't wait to see what Salem had in store for me.

Almost every Halloween since I was a kid, I've wanted to be a witch, and our new city seemed like the perfect place to live out the dream daily. Each year, the entire month of October is one big Halloween party... with around 250,000 of your closest, weirdest (in the best way) friends. It's a bit like attending Mardi Gras in New Orleans— a month-long celebration that welcomes tourists from all over the world.

The rest of the year, Salem is quaint and beautiful. I fell in love with the energy of the small town and the ability to walk everywhere we wanted to go. Cobblestone streets lead to intimate restaurants, cozy coffee shops, and mystical metaphysical stores. Everywhere you look, it's spilling over with witchery. There are sprawling parks and beaches, a wharf and historic old lighthouse, centuries-old cemeteries, and just *so. much. history.*

Salem was colonized in 1626, and was named Naumkaeg after the indigenous people who lived there. It was changed to Salem, short for Jerusalem, meaning "City of Peace," shortly after. Ironic name for a place most well-known for the Witch Trials of 1692, a time that was anything but peaceful.

Long before Salem, during the "Burning Times," (the dark ages of 19th century Europe) there were healers called pagans— a word meaning "country dweller." These were women who lived in rural locations far from the city. The pagans were steeped in nature, made medicines out of herbs in their cauldrons, assisted in childbirth, and generally functioned as the medicinal leaders in their community. Frequently they were also seen as spiritual leaders, which led them to be seen as a threat by the church. Rumors and propaganda began to spread. Stories were told about how these witches' potions would turn your skin green and give you warts, and they were portrayed with a pointed hat to discredit them as dunces. It was said that they worked for the devil. Fears about witchcraft escalated. Hysteria.

It's estimated that 60,000 people were burned at the stake, most of them women.

Fast forward to the Salem Witch Trials of 1692. A reverend's daughter and niece both came down with a mysterious illness that caused them to scream and flail on the ground with inexplicable seizures. The doctor during that time had very limited knowledge, so when he couldn't come up with a cause, it was decided that the patients— in this case the two girls— must be bewitched. Any mention of witchcraft in these puritan times caused panic because there was such a fear of the devil. Thus began the Witch Trials. Women who were considered social outcasts, or those who were least able to defend themselves, were the first accused. A slave from Barbados was suspect because she was dancing with the girls in the woods days prior, and a very impoverished single woman was next. The first victim hanged was a woman known to not attend church, who owned a tavern.

Over 200 people were accused, 19 were hanged, at least 4 died in prison awaiting trial, and one man was pressed to death.

Salem today has a very high population of Pagans and Wiccans. Modern day witches. Healers. So what does all that have to do with me?

During the years I spent in Salem, I learned that I am a healer. I am a witch. I stand with these women and I carry their spirits with me. And through them, I began to learn how to be authentically me, to live a life full of love and not fear. And I learned there are many people on the same journey as I am. Artists, musicians, mediums, energy-, light-, and bodyworkers. Those who unselfishly heal others, and are almost always under some kind of scrutiny and judgment for it by those who fear. Whether it be religious judgment, judgment from our families who think we should "get a real job," or just neighbors who think we're weird.

We, as a society, are still in the dark ages, but as the saying goes, "there is no light without darkness." I'm here to shine and to help others do the same.

I applied for a job leading tours at the Salem Witch Village. Up until that point, I wasn't comfortable with public speaking, and I thought that perhaps speaking in front of many people day after day would stop my face from turning bright red and my mind from going blank. I started learning about the fascinating, dark history of Salem, and my fear of public speaking subsided. Instead, I was excited to share these horrifying stories with the masses.

During my first October in Salem, I would drag a speaker with a microphone on a rolling hand-truck through the streets of Salem with about 50 tourists on a Candlelit Ghostly Tour. Each guest would hold a taper candle with a plastic cup cut to top it so that the candle didn't blow out or drip wax on the tourist's hand.

During one of the numerous tours I did over that first October, when my tour arrived in front of the location of the Witch Dungeons of 1692 (it was just an office building by then), I was talking about the horrendous conditions and the people who died there awaiting trial. And a woman's cup on her candle just popped off and fell on the ground. Weird. I wondered to myself if this was a spirit showing up for my tours each night. Another night, another cup would fall off. Sometimes tourists would drop their cameras, but insist that it felt like someone, or something, knocked it out of their hand. This phenomena would happen so often that I could say, "And now, someone's cup will pop off their candle." And, of course, it did.

At the next stop on the tour, I would talk about how the leading paranormal investigation television shows had filmed episodes and investigated the restaurant located at the original site of the homestead and tavern of the first accused witch, Bridget Bishop. Tourists would ask me if I knew anyone in town that would take *them* on an investigation. I didn't know any local paranormal societies, but after being asked at the conclusion of almost every tour, I decided to look into it.

The Victorian
Mansion

My friend Corey and I joined a paranormal team called New England GHOST. At long last, I purchased my very own KII meter, an audio recorder, a few other gadgets and tools, and started learning how to investigate. The first investigation we got to participate in was the Sylvester K. Pierce Victorian Mansion in Gardner, Massachusetts— the ninth most haunted house in the country. Gardner is a little over an hour drive from Salem, and we were buzzing the whole way with excitement and adrenaline, not to mention the energy drinks we'd drunk to ensure a wide-awake investigation. The mansion was enormous. Stunning, intricate Victorian detail graced every corner. Unfortunately, I hear it's been turned into a haunted tourist attraction in recent years (fun, totally strange, fact: it seems to be owned by a group affiliated with the carnival hip-hop group Insane Clown Posse), but when Corey and I investigated, it was still a private residence. We met with the homeowner, who took us on a tour of each room, telling us about the paranormal activity most common for each individual space.

After the short tour concluded, it was lights out.

Did you know it's actually best to investigate while it's dark? Television shows don't just do it to make it feel creepier. Darkness limits EMF contamination, but perhaps even more importantly, it's best to turn the lights off and make sure it's very quiet because your natural senses are heightened in the dark. You might see a shadow or hear a noise that you wouldn't normally if you were going about your evening with the lights on and laughing with your friends. For those wondering whether the darkness leads to overactive imaginations, I invite them to go on an investigation of their own, lights out. See for yourself.

We took turns investigating each room in pairs. We started with the basement. There was a bar next door blasting its music, and the sound seemed to reverberate most into the basement. Unsurprisingly, with all the booming noise, we didn't experience much activity there. We moved on to one of the upstairs bedrooms called the Red Room. We set our KII meter on the bed and started asking questions. The meter responded quickly when we asked questions about a woman, but it wasn't consistent. We decided to set up a flashlight on the dresser.

"Will you turn that flashlight on for us please?" I asked.

The flashlight turned on instantly. Perhaps the entity we were working with had an easier time working with the flashlight — during investigations, it's common that different equipment works for different encounters.

"Thank you. Can you turn it off please?"

The flashlight turned off instantly.

"Do you like me?" Corey asked

Flashlight on.

"Do you like me?" I asked.

Flashlight off.

Everyone went around the room, asking if we were liked by this spirit. The flashlight would respond instantly to each of us, except for one investigator. She said something like, "Why? What did I do?" And we all laughed. The flashlight turned on.

"If you like laughter in your home, please turn the flashlight off."

Flashlight off.

Perhaps this spirit was playing games with us and thought he or she was pretty funny.

We investigated the rest of the evening without many more significant events, but it was an amazing experience.

We continued investigating other private homes and businesses with the team: a beach house in Maine with claims of a full body apparition; the attic of a home in New Hampshire with voices of a child being heard at night; an old warehouse in Beverly with claims of seeing shadows and noises; and a small townhome in Salem with claims of frequently encountering the spirit of an older Mormon woman who didn't like the homeowner's new age books and would throw them off the shelves. (We caught an EVP at that home with the words "No wine!")

The Cowboy

A concerned mother in Salem called us because her kids wouldn't sleep in their own bed. They would only sleep on her floor. She said that her kids kept seeing the ghost of an old cowboy in their kitchen. A cowboy? In Salem, Massachusetts? Sounded like an interesting investigation. We always invited the client to join us for the evening, in opposition to what they do on ghost hunting TV shows. We spent some time in the attic, the bedrooms, and the living room, and then moved on to the kitchen. We sat around a small dining room table with our equipment laid out in front of us, and started out with the standard questions:

"If anyone is here with us tonight, we'd love to speak to you. The kids in this house are afraid of you and we would just like to know who you are so we can assure them that you are no one to be afraid of. Please light up one of our meters if you're here."

Instantly, the KII meter shot to red.

"Thank you. If you are a man, can you turn on the meter again?"

KII to red.

"Thank you. Do you know you are scaring the kids in this house? Please light up the meter if you do not mean to scare the kids."

KII to red.

"We have an audio recorder here. Could you tell us your name?"

When we listened back to the recorder, we could distinctly hear the name "Jim."

We did a little research and found out that the previous home-owner was named Jim. And after talking to the neighbor one day, we were told that Jim would dress up as a cowboy every year for Halloween.

Jim did not mean to scare the kids. We speculate that he was just always around and never knew how or when the kids would be able to see him. We told him that either he needed to go, or he should always walk around with a smile so the kids wouldn't be afraid of him. In general, spirits aren't scary, just misunder-stood.

A few days later, we came back to cleanse the house with the kids using sage. I love getting kids involved in clearing a space. I explained how cleansing works. From a scientific standpoint, the properties of sage actually neutralize positive ions. Too many positive ions in and around our body is what makes some-thing feel like "bad energy," causing stress, fatigue, and irrita-tion. Burning sage and releasing negative ions makes the space, and our bodies, feel lighter and clear.

I really feel that intention and visualization help to clear the air even more. In the case of a spirit in your home, the spirit is just like any other negative energy that is not welcome there. All energy is the same, whether it was someone who crossed over, or it's your own energy left from an argument with your hus-band in your bedroom. You want to clear it. When my family has all been sick with the flu, I use Clorox wipes on all surfaces, then I want to sage. I want all the negative, sick energy to leave. Smudging uses the elements of mother nature: Earth=Sage. Smoke= Fire, A seashell to hold the sage= Water, and a feather= air to blow the smoke where you want to clear. So, you open all windows in your home, and as you burn the sage, you are envisioning the smoke wrapping itself around the energy and carrying it out the window. And as I said before, this works really well with kids. I involve them and let them hold the feather and blow the smoke under their beds, in their closet, up in an attic, wherever scares them. It's amazing how freeing this is for them. This is a powerful form of magick.

Old Town Hall

I t was amazing to me that businesses in Salem didn't like to be associated with being haunted. Why not?! Salem is the Halloween capital of the United States. People flock there for a scare. You would think that having a spirit in your establishment would be good for business. But we were met with push back, not open arms, when we tried to speak with locals about investigating downtown businesses.

Old Town Hall was the first business to allow us to investigate, but for a hefty price. The hall is rented out for many different types of events such as weddings, concerts, performances, and other private functions. So we just decided to rent the space for the evening just like any other party planner, open it to the public, and charge a per-person fee for the investigation to make up the cost. We had many investigators from our paranormal society join us to help with the crowd.

We began our evening giving our attendees the history of Old Town Hall, a lesson in using our ghost hunting equipment, and the paranormal claims of the building. We set up laser grids on the entire second floor in hopes that a shadow or apparition would walk in front of it and block the light. We also set up cameras throughout the building to catch activity.

Then we turned off the lights and split up into groups of about

4 or 5 people each. I took my group to an upstairs restroom because I always thought I saw motion or a shadow up there in the window when I would pass by at night on my walk home. I was actually surprised that the window belonged to a bathroom. I sat on the floor with my group in a circle with some EMF detectors on the floor between us.

"Hello!" I said. "I think I've seen you many times from the window when I was outside below. I'm here to talk to you and I have many different types of equipment here that will help you talk to me. If you touch one of them, they will light up and tell us that you're here. They won't hurt you. I promise."

I really don't know how or why I knew, but I felt that I was talking to a little boy. I didn't share these thoughts with anyone, though. I wasn't sure how I would I explain that this felt like a little boy's energy in the room. I'm a paranormal investigator. I use scientific equipment. I'm not a medium. I don't do this by feeling. This was new for me.

"If you're here with us, can you turn on the meter for me please?"

Nothing.

"Can you tell me your name? If you talk really loudly into this recorder, we can listen back to it and we might be able to hear you."

Silence.

We sat and tried a little bit more but I felt that he wasn't there anymore. Again, I have no idea why I suddenly knew that.

We decided to leave the restroom and join another group that was in the main hall. We quietly walked in and sat down to listen. They were getting amazing flashlight play.

"Were you on trial for practicing witchcraft?" One of our team members asked. "You can shut the light off. We aren't going to hurt you."

The flashlight turned off.

"Thank you," he said.

One of our attendees said, "This is the room where they do re-enactments of the trials."

The flashlight turned on.

"He agreed with me," he laughed.

"Do you watch the actors as they act out the scenes of the trials?"

The flashlight turned off.

"Thank you. Were you hanged?"

The flashlight turned on.

"Thank you."

The flashlight didn't respond to any other questions after that. We sat for a bit, waiting. I watched the laser grid on the wall. All seemed quiet. I suddenly had an idea. I had a tennis ball in my bag and wondered if a little boy would want to play with a ball. So I took my group to the first floor and I put the ball and a KII meter on top of the counter of the gift shop. Suddenly, I could feel a presence.

"Hello!" I said again. "I brought you a ball! Would you like to play with me?"

We all stared intently at the ball.

"It moved!" Someone said.

I didn't see anything. We all cocked our heads and stared at it.

It rolled slightly.

There were collective gasps, and ooos and aaahs.

"Thanks for playing with me! We saw you move the ball! That was awesome! Can you touch the meter next to the ball and make it light up?"

The KII meter flickered.

"Thank you! Now, just so we know it's you, can you move the lights all the way to red three times? Like, 1... 2... 3..." I pointed and motioned which direction the lights would move.

The meter lit up to red. 1...2...3 times exactly as I asked.

Everyone yelled "Wow!" at the same time.

"Sorry we're excited. That was the most amazing KII hit we'd ever seen! Thank you so much!" I beamed. "Are you a girl? Can you light up the meter if you are a girl?"

The light stayed on green.

"Ok. If you are a boy, can you light up the meter?"

The light instantly lit all the way to red.

"*I knew it!*" I thought. "*How do I know that?*"

We received a few more responses and then the connection died down a bit.

We went back upstairs to join the other groups. My friend Corey was sitting on some bleachers with two girls I didn't know.

"This is Jen and Holly. They are both psychics and own a tarot shop in town. They were both telling me that they feel the presence of a little boy here."

"*Whoa. That's crazy.*" I thought. And my surprise must have shown on my face because they all looked at me like, "What?"

We chatted a little bit about the pressures of starting a business in Salem, and we also talked to Holly about the ghost tour that she did part-time for another neighboring company during October. Next, we talked about how the cemeteries in Salem feel— how their energy is different from other cemeteries. We spent some more time investigating with them for the evening, and when it got late and it was time to pack up and go, we cleansed all of our attendees with sage and thanked everyone for coming. Our team never found anything else on video or audio from that evening.

Corey and I became good friends with Holly and Jen. They were really awesome people, and we all thought it would be great to have psychics on our team to help investigate around town. I was also excited that I might be able to learn more about how to use my intuition from them. It had been a very long time since I even thought about it. It was like little flashes in my brain went, *"You used to do this!"*

The Lyceum

We were dying to investigate at 43 Church Street, which stands on the land that used to be owned by Bridget Bishop, the first woman accused of witchcraft during the trials of 1692. We had heard footsteps outside in the alley during the candlelit tours, and tourists frequently saw a woman standing in the window. I was really excited to spend an evening collecting my own evidence.

Corey, Holly, Jen, and I held an event there together. Jen and Holly advertised their tarot business, and I was beginning to tell people about the tour company I was in the early stages of starting. After the restaurant closed, we were able to turn the lights off and investigate on our own. We were joined by a few other friends who were equally thrilled at the opportunity to spend a couple hours ghost hunting there. We went upstairs and did our usual sweep with our EMF detectors to see which areas of the building have "normal" EMF. Then we set our meters down on a round table and set chairs around it.

After lights out, we started asking questions.

"Hi. We know you have groups come in all the time excited to talk to you, so you've probably seen this equipment before. If you're here, could you turn on one of these meters?"

Nothing.

We asked a few more questions and the meters were not responding. Suddenly, we heard a "Bang!" come from the kitchen. There had been claims here of glasses flying off the bar, so a pan or pot in the kitchen wasn't entirely out of the question. Corey and I went to the kitchen with a Mel Meter to see what had made the noise while the rest of the group stayed seated. We walked around the corner and peered into the kitchen, dimly lit by the red flashlight of our Mel Meter. It was empty and nothing seemed amiss.

"Hey! The KII meter is flashing!" our friend Kevin said. As soon as we came back into the room, the meter stopped responding. We asked a few more questions and did not receive a response. I noticed a shadow by the stairwell and walked over to investigate. As soon as I left the table, the KII meter lit up.

"It's playing with us!" Kevin said.

The meter lit up and we laughed.

"Well, this might be the little girl who is rumored to haunt the building. Maybe she's having fun. I'll walk away and see if we get another response." I said.

As soon as I walked to the other end of the room, the meter flashed again. I walked back to the meter and asked, "Hey Bridget Bishop, is that you?"

Nothing.

"Are you playing with us?" Kevin asked.

Again, the meter flickered.

"See! Playing!!" he said.

I definitely did not feel the energy of an older woman. This felt like a girl to me. I asked Holly and Jen who they felt here, and they agreed.

We spent the rest of the evening investigating in different rooms: the kitchen, downstairs, the restrooms. We didn't really get anything until I was standing in front of a mirror and Corey said she was going to take my picture. "If you're here, can you show up in the picture next to Kim?"

She clicked her camera, looked down at her screen and screamed, "Whoa!"

"What did you get?" I asked excitedly.

She turned the screen toward me, and directly over my right shoulder was a big white orb. Now, I'm not usually an "orb person." I believe that most orbs tourists find in their photographs are most likely dust. But this particular orb showed up right when she asked. So what is an orb exactly? A built up ball of energy perhaps? A spirit manifesting in the best way they can? I believe that if you see an orb with your own eyes and not a camera, it is more likely to be some type of spirit energy. If you feel a loved one with you during a special event, such as a wedding, and your wedding photos come back and there is an orb over your shoulder in multiple photographs, it was most likely your family member.

Who stood next to me in that photo that evening? Bridget Bishop? A little girl? That was the only evening I ever had the chance to investigate at 43 Church. I loved the energy there. Definitely nothing negative. If I had the means, I would have purchased the entire building and spent most of my time investigating there. It was magic.

Paranormal Salem

I was a wife and mother, I was in grad school, I was working part time giving ghost tours, and I was spending a couple evenings a week as a paranormal investigator. To say I was busy is an understatement. But, I figured I might as well add to my plate and start a business before October began in Salem again.

Corey and I drove to Warwick, Rhode Island to attend a weekend training with TAPS Academy. We geeked out being in the office of the Ghost Hunters and took many selfies. Our instructors for the weekend were not Jason or Grant, but amazing investigators nonetheless. I took avid notes. We learned everything from the history of ghost hunting dating back to 7AD to quantum physics.

After investigating as many places in Salem as we were able, we were ready to create Paranormal Salem. The name came easy. I had a friend help with the vision I had for a logo, then we created a website, signed up for a google voice number that ended in HUNT, and I placed an ad in Salem's Haunted Happenings brochure with instructions to meet at the Witch Trials Memorial at 10pm, later than any other tour company. I didn't want to compete with anyone.

I created a tour. With help from my theatre background, I wrote a script. It included Salem's history and paranormal activity, the history of ghost hunting, instructions on how to use the various pieces of scientific equipment I had invested in, and even a few jokes. I would take care of my son, go to school or work, and then work again until past midnight. There was an interest in our tours right away. I decided to cap the attendees to 20 people per tour to make sure it felt more intimate than the other tours in town.

The first October of owning the company was busy, hectic, exhilarating, and exhausting, and I loved every second of it. I would get up around 6am, grab bagels for the crew in the Haunted Neighborhood, which included the Witch Village, Wax Museum, Frankenstein's Laboratory Haunted House, the Candlelit Ghostly Tour, and the Witching Hour Spell Casting. I would run around all day as a manager, helping out where needed and running the huge amounts of money to deposit in the safe in the office. I ate junk food from the nearby businesses and food booths, and sometimes the general manager's mom would cook homemade empanadas for us. When it got dark, I'd refresh my makeup, throw a gothic-looking skirt over my jeans, and take a few Candlelit Tours around town. Each tour was about a mile. We would close up, count the money for the day, and then I would head next door to the Witch Trials Memorial to begin my Paranormal Salem tour. Start all over and do it again the next day.

I'd even spend time on my few days off editing weekly YouTube videos for our tourists. My degree in Sound Design really helped with this, especially while enhancing our EVPs. My thought was that if each person ended up in a souvenir video with crazy paranormal evidence, they would share those videos with their friends and more people would hear of us and book a tour. It worked. Our first October was such a success that I wanted to make it even better the next year. I started taking a few business classes and workshops at Salem State University around the time I graduated from Emerson. We had planned to move back home to Seattle, but with a growing business, we decided to stick around.

I started subleasing a small office space from a counselor who never needed her office past the afternoon. It worked out amazingly. The office was at 30 Church Street, the building that used to be Salem's first firehouse. The connection between a firehouse and Ghostbusters was completely lost on me until a fellow tour guide pointed it out one day and laughed. It was wonderful to have a space aside from my dining room table to edit videos, listen to EVP's etc. It was especially great to have an office so that my business address was no longer my apartment. I could take tourists to an actual space at the end of the evening and offer hot cocoa at the end of cold nights. I could also sell a few things.

But the best reason to have this office space was that the entire building was empty at midnight when we were there ending our tours, and it had a basement that was a big open, empty, creepy space. On rainy evenings, it was wonderful to have an indoor space to investigate. We didn't know then that the old firehouse was haunted. It just met our needs at the time. Because of my tours and my publicity, it is now a known haunted building.

My goal with my tours was to give people that personal paranormal experience that I craved before I purchased my first KII meter and became a ghost hunter myself. I wanted these ghost hunting shows you see on television to come to life, and I wanted to turn skeptics into believers. But I never rigged anything to go off on its own. I didn't have someone hiding in the bushes ready to jump out at someone. (That happened to us on a cheesy ghost tour of Prague once.) The only time I audibly gasped and made my attendees jump was when a skunk came strolling toward us from the cemetery one evening. If nothing paranormal happened, my clients would at least learn Salem and paranormal history, and have a great time trying. I didn't know then that there would never be an evening where absolutely nothing happened. During a successful summer of tours,

I decided to hire two more tour guides. My company ended up with a fascinating and unique perspective as we investigated the same places night after night with different people. As my tour guides compared evidence with each other, it was amazing that we were catching the same activity, and the same names on the audio recorder each tour.

Walk With Me

The spirits of Salem were very keen to communicate with us, however, surprisingly, we don't believe we ever communicated directly with an accused witch of 1692. The following is my Paranormal Salem tour script—including all of my favorite history of this spooky town. I hope that you can imagine walking the streets of Salem with me and feel the energy that lingers there:

My tour began at the Witch Trials Memorial. I would introduce myself to the nervous, excited group and explain some of the ground rules, which included silencing cell phones and not smoking. Smoke would cause ghostly images on camera and I wanted our paranormal photos to be as authentic as possible. I always encouraged people in these groups to take as many pictures and audio/video as they wished during the tour— using their own devices as well as my own— because you never know what someone will catch!

The main focus of my tour was to take the fear out of the unknown, and to give visitors the most accurate information possible. I would be sharing ghost stories and urban legends of the area, but was very clear to distinguish accurate historical facts vs. legends. I debunked a lot of ghost stories that tourists might have already heard about Salem while on other tours. But first, at the beginning of each tour, I would train my group how to use my investigation equipment and metaphysical tools, starting with Dowsing Rods.

Dowsing has been around for centuries. It has been used for finding water and other natural elements. It has been used by oil refineries, farmers, well drillers, treasure hunters, police detection, and even used by the military during World War II for finding land mines. Everything in the universe is a mass of molecules that vibrates and has an energy field. This energy vibrates in waves, which can be measured. By loosely holding a dowsing rod in each hand, one can pick up and detect these fields as they cross or move to detect physical manifestations that require an amount of energy. Whether it's picking up on the energy of an underground powerline, or an invisible ghost standing in front of you... sometimes it's hard to know. However, after personally spending years measuring the energy around Salem, I was confident that I knew the difference between "normal" and "para-normal" energy. One of my favorite things about dowsing rods is that they cannot experience battery drain like an EMF meter.

My absolute favorite tool is a pendulum. They work the same way as a dowsing rod, picking up those same energy vibrations. Hold the small bead of the pendulum, called the fob, between your index finger and thumb, and let it swing above the open palm of your other hand. Always ask your pendulum to show you "yes" and "no." Don't ever let someone else tell you which is which. It's a personal thing and it's going to be different for the individual. It may even be different each time you use the same pendulum. For instance, "yes" could make a circle, "no" could swing back and forth. For ghost hunting, you can use it to ask the spirit questions. I will explain many more ways to use a pendulum later in this book.

A KII meter is the most popular battery-operated EMF meter for paranormal investigation. The meter is used to detect Electro-Magnetic Fields, and was— and still is— first used by electricians to test electrical breaker boxes and bad wires. EMF is human-made energy. Cellphones, televisions, and any electronic device gives off EMF. Too much of this energy can cause all sorts of symptoms including paranoia, a general "creepy" feeling, and even sickness and nausea. It is common for someone to sense a presence in their basement, when in reality, they're sensing old wiring. I once had a client who would feel and see spirits in their bedroom at night. Upon investigation, I learned that their alarm clock was putting off high amounts of EMF. Removing the bad alarm clock removed the sense of spirits. No ghost busting needed! However, when ghost hunting, the theory is that a spirit can use this human-made energy to make themselves known. Spirits are able to light up the meter and communicate.

There are many different types of EMF detectors. Another popular one is a "Ghost Meter," which is less expensive than a KII meter and great for beginner investigators. It measures the same ElectroMagnetic Field as a KII, but uses a needle to indicate the presence of energy rather than glowing colored lights. When the needle of the Ghost Meter jumps between 2.0 and 7.0, it is indicative of a nearby energy source and will beep and light up, whereas the KII uses LED lights green, yellow, red, and orange and is silent. It's great to put in another room and wait for an electronic sound when you know no one is in there.

A Mel Meter is a three-in-one investigation tool. The man who invented it had a daughter named Melanie who passed away, and he wanted to try to contact her, hence the name "Mel" meter. It has a digital readout for the EMF detector so it will fluctuate slightly on its own. If it goes any higher than a .2, then you might have something interesting going on. It also has a red flashlight for help with your night vision when you're on a dark investigation. It also tells you the ambient temperature of the room. There are other infrared thermometers and temperature guns that are very directional and used to detect "cold spots" which could be a spirit trying to manifest itself.

A Spirit Box, also known as a Ghost Box or Dialog Box, scans through AM and FM radio frequencies, making white noise. It is a theory that a spirit can manipulate the energy of this "static" and communicate through it. It's like real time communication being able to hear a word and respond right away.

I carry a Digital Audio Recorder to record EVP, which stands for Electronic Voice Phenomena. EVP's were first discovered in the 1950's. A man was out in the forest, recording bird songs, and when he listened to the recording, he could hear what sounded like the voice of his deceased father saying his name. We now know that audio recorders will pick up voices that the human ear can't hear at the time.

I had a few other tools that I would sometimes use. One was a device called a Lux meter, which detects subtle changes in the light level in an investigative area. It can pick up orbs and any other light source that our eyes can't see. I also had a Laser Grid, which I would use at the end of the tour in the basement of the old firehouse building. It would shine a grid of green light on the back wall and corners of the room. If any of the lights in a section went out, it could mean that a spirit, or at least an intense build-up of energy, had blocked the light.

Lastly, on each of my tours, I would record video using a night vision camcorder to film my guest investigators, and then edit and upload souvenir videos for YouTube. As I said before, it was a great way for my newly trained investigators to show their friends any evidence we caught on film, and also help advertise my tours. Win-win.

Personal experiences were the most valuable evidence of all. I always reminded everyone to keep their senses open for smells, a feeling of cobwebs on your skin, or feelings of being watched and general uneasiness.

After explaining what each piece of equipment did, I spoke about the history of Salem Massachusetts beginning with The Witch Trials Memorial:

"The Witch Trials Memorial was designed by a holocaust survivor who believed that anyone harmed in the injustice of others deserves a memorial. It was erected in 1992 to mark the tercentennial of the Witch Trials. There are 19 benches along the stone walls for each person who was hanged, and one for Giles Corey, who was pressed to death for not entering a plea. It's a common misconception that the accused witches are buried here or in the Charter Street Cemetery on the other side of the wall. All of the accused were thrown in a mass grave, near the execution site where they were hanged. The execution site is believed to be where Gallows Hill Park stands today, but no one knows for sure, since the great Salem fire destroyed all public records in 1914, not to mention, the city has always attempted to pretend such harrowing events never happened."

Side note: In 2017, a group of researchers from Salem State University "confirmed" the location of the executions, which lines up perfectly with my intuition and historical research that I have done. They had some fancy "ground-penetrating radar," which is apparently better than just using your own intuition. Locals have always known and felt where it was located on Proctor's Ledge, otherwise known as "above the Walgreens." However, the burial site has not yet been located because this equipment shows the earth was not deep enough for a mass grave.

"The Witch Trials Memorial is bordered on two sides by the Charter Street Cemetery or "Old Burying Point." This is the second oldest cemetery in the United States. The city will not allow visitors into the cemetery after dark, which we absolutely abide by. I definitely don't want these ancient headstones being damaged while investigating in the dark. The sign out front says 1637, but the city got the date wrong, as the oldest headstone inside dates 1628. Judge John Hathorne, the famous "hanging judge" during the witch trials and great-great grandfather of author Nathaniel Hawthorne, is buried here. (Notice he added a "W" to his name to disassociate himself from his ancestor.) *Also, Mary Corey, Giles Corey's first wife, is buried here, along with witnesses to the trials and accused witches*

who were released before execution. People end up with very strange photos in this cemetery. Shadow figures, strange lights, mists and orbs. Many people see a woman in white, who is believed to be Mary Corey trying to get to the Howard Street Cemetery, down the street where Giles is buried. We also have heard some strange disembodied voices on our recorders from time to time out here.

The Samuel Pickman house borders the memorial on the third side. The house was built around 1664 and it is Salem's oldest remaining house. There are many ghost stories surrounding this house. Legend has it that a man killed his wife and daughter here before killing himself. I have not found any proof that happened here. Some say this might have happened next door in the plot of land where the Witch Trials Memorial is, since a house once stood here. The tree that stands in the center of the memorial is clouded in many rumors. Some relate to the legend of this family and that perhaps this man hanged himself on this tree. Another rumor is that a child fell from the tree and died in recent years, but I have never been able to find tangible evidence of this either. Many tourists mistakenly assume this tree is where the accused witches were hanged back in 1692, which is also wholly untrue. There are many claims of seeing faces in the windows at night and a candle burning in the upstairs window of the Pickman House. During my investigations, we were able to debunk that. The "candle" that people claim to see is the reflection of a street lamp, and the faces seen in the glass is due to the warped, cloudy condition and mineral deposits of the original windows from the 1600's."

In my years of investigating, there was one photo from the memorial that really stands out as unique and definitely paranormal. A blurry, translucent woman in a white dress was seen sitting on one of the benches in a tourist's photo. I can tell you first-hand that there was no one anywhere near that bench when she snapped the picture. She looked like a beautiful, serene spirit who stopped by to enjoy the energy there for a moment. I truly understand the love of the energy in the memorial. I would sit on the edge of the wall some summer nights by myself, staring off into the dark cemetery, and sometimes closing my eyes and sitting very still, just feeling like I was welcomed by spirits and belonged in this city.

Guests on my tour would spend time feeling the energy and conducting their own investigations using my supplied equipment. I would stand by and be available for questions and advice. Surprisingly, after everyone got over the initial, "Wow! This thing is so cool!" feeling using the EMF detectors, everyone decided they most loved using a pendulum. Giving people the ability to use their own intuition in a city that was so full of amazing energy was the best gift.

Next, we would walk to Old Town Hall:

"The Old Town Hall is the earliest surviving municipal structure in Salem, dating back to 1816. The second floor, called the Great Hall, has always been used as a public hall, and contained town offices until 1837. The first floor was used as a public market. Today it is used as a free Salem History Museum, and they do re-enactments of the witch trials, called "Cry Innocent," on the second floor. The Old Town Hall is located in Derby Square, named for Elias Derby, America's first millionaire. He owned the first trade ship to sail over to China and the West Indies. The street closest to Old Town Hall is called Front Street because Elias Derby had a waterfront home here. The land is now filled in and the waterfront is much further east. Derby also had two homes near Pickering Wharf—one is still standing, but the one that used to stand here was his last home, and he died here. (I would joke that I had yet to contact Mr. Derby to have him help me make millions too.)

Since many tour groups in town claim to see a little boy in that top window peering out at them at night, our team spent an evening investigating inside Old Town Hall a few months ago, and it's a very active location. The show "Paranormal State" filmed here once. We got a lot of flashlight play with someone we believe was a little boy, and also from someone who answered us when we asked if they liked watching the reenactments of the trials, and that they themselves were hanged. We also had flashlights and tennis balls move on their own when asked, and we got the most impressive KII hit we'd ever seen. In the gift shop area, the KII meter started going crazy flashing. We asked, "If that's you, could you please turn that off?" And the meter instantly went back to a single green light. We then asked, "Could you make it go all the way to red 3 times?" And instantly it did it...1, 2, 3."

These tales elicited a collective shiver from the group.

We would spend a little time investigating Derby Square, and I would tell my group to make sure to take photos of the windows, and also keep their eyes out for an old woman in a brown dress. She was another urban legend, seeing her wandering outside this area, but I had yet to see her.

We never did find evidence of this woman, but I do believe that I met the little boy who roams the building when we spent the evening investigating inside. What I remember most about investigating *outside* on the steps of Old Town Hall was repeatedly hearing the name "Paul" on our audio recorder each night. All of my tour guides heard this name, over and over, and without knowing or consulting with each other. It was a busy tourist season and we didn't have a lot of time to connect and compare evidence, so it was amazing to find out that all of us had made contact with a man named Paul at Old Town Hall.

Next, we would walk to a building with amazing history at 43 Church Street. On the way, the elevator doors inside the Salem Green building would sometimes open on their own if someone asked on active nights. When finally arriving at the closed, dark restaurant, I would tell my attendees about the history of this land:

"43 Church Street was previously called The Lyceum (not sure what it's called today, but it's probably a restaurant. It seems to change owners quite frequently). *It was once used as a lecture hall —hence the name Lyceum, and was built in 1830. Most notably, Alexander Graham Bell, from Boston, made the first public telephone*

call to his friend Thomas Watson in this building in 1877 during a public lecture. People were pretty shocked about this. They considered this new device black magic, and it was thought you could use the telephone to contact the dead.

Long before that famous phone call took place, this land used to be owned by Bridget Bishop. Her homestead, tavern, and a rumored apple orchard were here. Bridget Bishop was the first person to be hanged during the witch hysteria. She wasn't very popular with the townspeople because she wore red dresses— not a very popular color for puritans at the time— had three husbands in her lifetime, and owned a tavern. She was probably a pretty cool lady! It is said that she haunts the Lyceum. People witness an apparition of a woman, especially on the second floor, glasses are moved or break on their own, and footsteps are heard. Televisions shows, "Ghost Hunters" (TAPS) investigated here, and also "Ghost Adventures". When TAPS was here, all of the computers turned on by themselves and one of them printed out a receipt at 1:13 A.M. saying "Good Morning." Employees in the building have never had that happen before."

On tours, we often recorded footsteps walking where we stood outside. People would be excited to show me photos of what looks like a woman peering out the window. However, after investigating inside and across the street at my office, I don't believe that it is a woman, but a little girl. We suspect that in the 1800's, there was a pond on this site and a little girl drowned. I believe that it is not Bridget Bishop, but a small playful girl who haunts this area. The photos of the "woman" peering out looks much more like a small girl than an older woman. And during our investigation, our KII meters would only react when we mentioned anything about playing with us. We believe she's a mischievous little girl showing up at parties and moving people's glasses, etc. She doesn't always stay at the Lyceum, but wanders over to the Old Firehouse building where my office was located across the street.

Next, we would head to the site of the old witch dungeons

where a modern office building now stands:

"The Old Witch Dungeon site is where the dungeons used to stand during the witch trials of 1692. Imprisonment here was a horrible experience. At least four people died here while awaiting trial because the conditions were so terrible. In 1956, the New England telephone company purchased the land here. While constructing the building that sits here now, the dungeons were discovered in the basement. It wasn't known where they were located until that time. Since there was unfortunately no historical society at the time, they just built over top of it. Employees hear shuffling, voices, and coughing when no one is down there, and apparently no one likes to be the last person in the building; they race out the door so they don't have to be the one to turn the lights off. Also, it is said that on the dates of the executions, the employees in the building hear screams and cries for help on the phone lines. It is rumored that they use their cell phones on those days each year. We've personally seen shadows in the windows and down the hall when no one is in the building. And we catch many, many EVP's here on our tours."

Usually, this would be the first time I would sit down to do an EVP session with a group. Even though my tour began the latest of any other tour in town, there were still many people walking past us on the cobblestone streets of downtown Salem while we investigated. This was a closed office building on the edge of town, away from most restaurants, so it was usually quiet enough to record.

"I will record the EVP session with an audio recorder as well as a night vision camcorder. It helps to rule out ambient noise when I listen back later when I can see all of the participants. We will now have everyone sit in a circle and be as quiet as possible. My number one rule is NO WHISPERING. If you want to say something to a spirit, or each other, say it out loud. Also, a yawn sounds a lot like "get out" during playback; and a deep inhale or sigh sounds like "help me." During an EVP session, if you happen to yawn, sniffle, or your stomach growls just tag it. Simply say "sniffle" or "stomach" out loud or

even just, "that was me." That way when I hear a creepy demon noise when I listen back, I'll know that someone was just hungry. It's also important to spit out gum and try your best to restrict movement so that clothing doesn't rub, or jewelry doesn't clank together. You have to be really careful debunking your audio just as much as your visual evidence."

I would then start the recorder, say the name of the place we were investigating, and the date and time of the session. We would then take turns asking questions, giving ample time between questions to hear an answer.

There are plenty of examples of what types of questions you can ask throughout this book, as I have written out many of my EVP sessions, but there are no rules about it. Listen to your intuition and ask what you feel. The major evidence we collected from the dungeon site included many EVPs. One that still stands out in my mind was one that clearly said, "It feels lonesome." The energy there always felt stifling and sad. I would never want to work in that building.

I would tell many other ghost stories to fill the time as I walked through the streets to each tour stop with my attendees. One of my favorites included the story of Giles Corey:

"During the trials, if you were accused of witchcraft, it didn't matter if you pleaded innocent or guilty, you would lose your home and all of your property. Giles was an old stubborn man. When he was accused, he refused to enter a plea one way or another. So he was taken to the land where the Howard Street Cemetery now sits to be tortured. Sheriff George Corwin forced him to lie on the ground with a huge plank of wood over his body—some say it was a large door. In an effort to force him to plea, heavy rocks were placed on top of the door. The Sheriff would ask, "How do you plead?" And Giles would say only, "More weight." It took him 3 days to die. His family fought to keep his property and eventually succeeded.

There's a well-known curse in Salem associated with Giles Corey. It is said that if you see his apparition wandering in the Howard Street

Cemetery, disaster will strike the city. He was said to have been seen before the Great Salem Fire of 1914, as well as some blizzards throughout the years. Additionally, there's a curse on any Sheriff of Salem. Corwin died of a heart attack just a few years after the trials, and every sheriff thereafter has either died or forced to resign due to a heart condition. Salem currently has no sheriff."

Another one of my favorite ghost stories to tell was the "Clue House." It was much too far to walk within the time constraints of the tour, but people loved to hear the story anyway:

"In 1830, an infamous murder took place in the Gardner-Pingree house, home of Captain Joseph White. He was struck in the skull by a pewter candlestick and then stabbed 13 times with a dagger. He was unmarried and lived with his niece, who also worked as his housekeeper. The murder was a huge shock to the community and is thought of as the first murder mystery case. Famous lawyer Daniel Webster presided over the case and eventually found that the Captain's great nephew hired hitman Richard Crowninshield to kill him for his fortune. The house is nicknamed the "Clue House" because it was Parker Brother's inspiration for the game Clue. Their factory was located just down the street in Salem. The murder also inspired writings by Nathaniel Hawthorne, who was a huge believer in the paranormal. He worked in the Custom House as a surveyor. In addition to writing The Scarlet Letter while on duty, he would also write about how he'd see ghosts wandering the halls at night when he was alone in the building, or hear ship captains discussing their treasures when no one was there.

In 1959, Richard Crowninshield's house was moved next door to Joseph White's house. It is said that is when the claims of paranormal activity began in the house. People believe that the crime spectrally repeats itself each year on the anniversary of the Captain's death. Also, people constantly claim to see him looking out the window from his mansion, watching the living outside."

The last stop on my tour was the basement of the Old Firehouse

30 Church Street:

"The building was Salem's first firehouse, built in 1861. We believe we have four ghosts here. The little girl that I mentioned at the Lyceum, we believe her name is Isabella, or her name starts with an L. An older man named John but goes by Jack who used to be a fire chief here, an older woman who died in her office upstairs in the 1980's. And also a dog! We've caught some great EVP's here in the basement as well as full conversations in our office upstairs. Once here in the basement, we heard a woman say "80" when I asked what year it was. We also caught it on our audio. We've seen shadows down here and we hear footsteps and chairs moving directly above us in Nick's Restaurant when no one is up there."

At the end of every tour, I would offer sage and sea salt to cleanse the space and our physical bodies before sending my newly trained paranormal investigators on their way. No one wanted a ghost to follow them home or to their hotel so they were very eager to learn about cleansing their energy. When each person had a small pile of sea salt in each hand, we would stand together, shoulder to shoulder in a circle and they would repeat after me, *"Your feet are firmly planted here, please do not follow."*

Forest River Park

I received an email from a woman saying she wanted to plan her best friend's bachelorette party by doing a private ghost hunt. She said the bride was a huge Ghost Hunters fan, and she found our tours by Google search when she came across an article written about Paranormal Salem on Boston.com that compared us to Jason Hawes and Grant Wilson. She said she wanted to do something longer than our regular tour around town. So Corey and I brainstormed, and we decided to take them to Forest River Park and then end their tour downtown. Forest River Park is a huge wooded area with a playground and beaches. It's also home to Pioneer Village, which is a living history museum of 17th century life. We had gotten some strange activity there on past investigations and took the opportunity to dive in further. Our evidence mostly consisted of strange photos. One shot near Pioneer Village looked like the apparition of a woman. In another instance, I was walking through the park and took a photo, and a small purple orb appeared. I instantly took another shot and the orb grew larger. The next photo, a larger purple orb that almost looked like it was the shape of a person. Another photo, it was gone. I was looking forward to going back for another visit.

We met the group in a pitch-black parking lot. I didn't know it at the time, but this girl did not tell the bride what their plans were for the evening. She joked that she thought they were going to be murdered when they pulled in. We explained how to use our ghost hunting equipment and started walking toward the playground in the middle of the park. They walked around with EMF detectors, occasionally one would blink for seemingly no reason and they were so excited to be out with us. We stopped at the playground to do an EVP session. We were all sitting around on one of the play structures asking the typical questions. "What's your name?" "How old are you?" etc., when we suddenly heard this small "squeak" sound.

"What was that?" one girl asked.

"It sounded like the swing." Corey said.

"Oh hell no!" another girl yelled.

"Oh it was probably just the wind." I said. But there was no wind.

We stopped the recorder to listen back to the sound and it indeed sounded like the swing moved. Corey walked over to the swing and pushed one, and then the other. She had this shocked look on her face, and I asked, "What is it? What's the matter?"

She replied, "This swing felt heavy. Like there was a child in it." She pushed the swing again and said that it no longer felt that way.

The girls attempted bravery and walked arm-in-arm closer to the swings to take some photos, and then we continued our EVP session.

"Are you a child?" I asked.

A few more questions and I hit the playback button. Very clearly we heard a male voice say, "Go home!" This group of women began screaming with a mix of fear and excitement. So, after we all calmed down a bit, we decided it was best to listen to this voice and head downtown.

We took the group to our usual downtown spots without too much activity. When we reached the site of the witch dun-

geons, they were giggling and having a great time as we con-
ducted our EVP session. When we listened back to the recorder,
we heard a man whisper, "Contain yourself." This time no one
screamed. They all laughed instead.

We heard from the girls a few days later by email with an
attached photo they took of the swings that night. It looked
like there was a shadow of a small child sitting in one of them.

Gallows Hill

One evening, we took a group up to Gallows Hill Park to investigate. Gallows Hill Park is named so because it is believed that the hanging site from the witch trials of 1692 was in that area. As mentioned before, there were no graves for these accused witches, as they were thrown in a mass grave near the gallows.

We parked our car near the baseball field and lifted our bags of equipment from the trunk. We had EMF detectors, audio recorders, and a night vision camera. There were four of us: me and Corey, one of our tour guides, Sydney, and friend of hers we'd never met.

Sydney's friend told us all that he was psychic and that he immediately felt the presence of a man from England. I don't know why but I got the "you're crazy" vibe from this guy and not a genuine intuitive. *"Yeah, okay dude."* I thought.

As we made our way across the field he says, "I can see orbs flying through the trees!"

I gave Corey the *"this guy is nuts"* look and she nodded her head. As I explained before, I believe that 99% of orbs can be completely debunked away.

I looked up to where he was pointing and I think my heart skipped a beat. "What the hell!" I yelled. "What is that?!"

I could see a huge ball of light dancing at the top of the tree line. I quickly grabbed my camera and snapped a shot. I looked down at my camera screen and I couldn't believe it—I actually caught it on film. I'd never seen anything like it. I knew right then that this was going to be an interesting evening.

After we all *ooh'd and aah'd* over the orb on my camera, we decided to head off toward the path that led up the hill into the woods. We began to walk slowly up the narrow path, turning on our flashlights as the lights from the neighborhood became dimmer.

So, I'm not going to lie. I didn't so much feel like the big bad ghost hunter that I thought I was. This guy kept saying that he always "sees a lot" and I guess I just didn't like his energy— Almost like he was bringing someone with us, like he had some sort of negative attachment. Corey felt the same way. We didn't speak about it right then, but I could tell. He said, "I feel like someone is behind us." Corey and I were bringing up the rear as we kept walking up the dark path. As if I wasn't freaked out enough, suddenly I could hear what sounded like footsteps behind us. Twigs breaking and leaves rustling. Corey heard it too, and we both locked arms as we kept walking, picking up our pace.

We continued to hear these noises as we walked. Our plan was to stop near the water tower high on the hill and stop to investigate there. This guy said he felt the presence of something further up and ran so far ahead of us that we just let him go. When he left, the noises in the forest stopped, further acknowledging my feelings that whatever this was, was attached to him personally.

We arrived at the water tower and found him sitting in the dark alone on a huge rock and he told us he saw the apparition of a man wearing a suit. This guy was creeping me out, but the energy here felt different. I started feeling back to my normal fearless self again and I was ready to investigate. We all sat on these big rocks and set out our EMF detectors and audio recorders. We asked multiple questions and we had no luck with any EMF. We took a few photos of the area with our new night vision camera, hoping something would show up, but we didn't see anything. With the mood and energy lightening a little, we decided to take a few selfies because the camera made our eyes glow. Sydney took a photo of Corey and I sitting on the boulder, and then we packed up and headed back down the trail. The hike back to the car was uneventful.

The next day, I put a few photos from our investigation on the business's Facebook page: The orb I caught in the trees, some shots of the woods, and the photo Sydney took of Corey and me on the boulder.

Someone commented, "It looks like there's a guy behind you!"

"I feel like someone is behind us." His words echoed in my head as I read the comment. I looked closely at the space between Corey and me... and I saw him. A distorted face with distinct eyes, nose, and mouth forming a half smile. His hair looked like it was sticking up in every direction. It even looked like he was wearing a skinny tie. The fact that Sydney's friend kept saying he was sensing a man and that he was behind us the whole evening; and we caught what looks like a man behind us on camera... it's really startling and validating. But even after all of those synchronicities, I still needed to attempt to debunk this photograph.

Corey and I set off to disprove this spirit photo a few nights later. We went back to Gallows Hill and sat down on the same rock, and brought a friend to take photos of us. We thought that maybe we would be able to see the rock behind us, that maybe there was the shape of a face in the rocks. But no, each picture showed nothing but blackness behind us. We also took photos of the rocks by themselves, up and down, thinking we might get a similar shape, but no luck. This was by far the best paranormal evidence I had caught yet— so great, in fact, that A&E saw it on our Facebook page and asked us to send in an audition tape for *My Ghost Story: Caught on Camera.*

My Ghost Story

Corey and I sent an audition video to A&E that included our photo of the man on Gallows Hill, and a few more of our favorite pieces of evidence, including the EVP's and photo from the bachelorette party at Forest River Park, and an apparition standing behind a tourist at the site of the witch dungeons.

We received a call from A&E saying they really liked our audition for *My Ghost Story: Caught on Camera.* They wanted to fly us to Los Angeles to have us on the show. I wanted to jump up and down and scream, but I contained myself (just like that spirit said to do). I knew that this opportunity could be really amazing for business, not to mention it would be a ton of fun.

We packed our bags a few weeks later and my husband drove us to the airport. Corey had never been to the west coast before so I was eager to introduce her to restaurants that weren't in Massachusetts. (I should mention that I was almost 5 months pregnant at the time. Satisfying my cravings was important!) We had asked A&E if they would allow us to fly in a couple days early to do some sightseeing and stay with a friend of mine and they agreed. We took in many tourist sights of LA: The Hollywood Walk of Fame, Rodeo Drive, we even visited Madame Tussaud's Wax Museum, and took a drive over to the La Brea Tar Pits. We were having an amazing time, and yes, pigging out at amazing restaurants.

A&E sent a car to pick us up and take us to the hotel they had booked for us. We were given a schedule for filming the next day. We would be picked up from the hotel at 3:30 p.m. I would be in hair and make-up at 4:00 p.m., and my interview would begin at 4:30 p.m. Corey would be in hair and make-up at 5:00 p.m., and her interview would begin at 5:30 p.m. *"Hair and make-up?! How cool! I feel like a movie star!"*

The next afternoon, I was spending far too much time prepping my own hair and make-up than was necessary, but I was worried I wouldn't like the way they were going to do it and hoped they wouldn't remove my hard work. I was also second-guessing my clothing. I was attempting to hide the fact that I was pregnant, but not wanting to look fat either. I was so nervous. Corey was nervous, too. My phone rang and we were told our car had arrived. We entered the elevator and ran into a couple who was also filming that day. They were also being picked up in our van, so we chatted about where we were from and a little about our ghost stories on the ride to the studio.

We arrived and were shown to the green room. There was a ton of delicious food all laid out for us to snack on: little sandwiches, veggie trays, fruit, cookies, brownies. For being a pregnant girl though, I wasn't feeling hungry. Nerves. They told us they were running a bit behind and to get comfortable. We sat down on one of the plush couches that were arranged in the center of the room and introduced ourselves to another storyteller who was waiting for her friend to finish her interview. This woman was also a paranormal investigator and told us that they lived in Florida. Everyone we talked to thought it was really neat that we lived in notoriously spooky Salem, Massachusetts.

I was called in to hair and make-up about a half hour later than scheduled. She told me that I could absolutely keep my make-up the way it was. She just added a little more powder to make my skin smooth and not shiny for the camera, and she added a little lipstick. She didn't do anything at all to my hair. One of the assistant producers arrived to walk me down to my interview. The hair and make-up woman came with us. He would repeat "Talent Walking" into his walkie-talkie as we continued down the hallway. *"Oh geez. Talent? Ha."*

When we reached the studio, my heart was pounding and my body has this awful habit of my cheeks turning red and it spreading all the way down my chest in splotches. (I always blamed it on being of Swedish descent, but who knows.) I thought I had conquered this feeling with as many tours and acting I had done at this point, but nothing prepared me for the nervousness I would feel when I walked into that room. There was a single chair with a bright blue backdrop surrounded by huge cameras on various rolling contraptions on the ground and above. There were quite a few people involved in production, including two people in the sound booth, camera operators, and other official-looking television staff, wearing earpieces and waiting for me. One man walked toward me and shook my hand.

"Hi! I'm Jason, the Production Manager. We've spoken on the phone. It's nice to meet you. We are going to start by having you sit down and all you're going to do is have a conversation with me to help calm down the nerves."

"Okay that sounds great." I said. I sat down in the chair and cameras started moving toward me. The make-up woman came over to touch up my face powder and arrange my necklace so it lay straight. Then he started with just conversational small talk about Salem. After a few minutes, I got into a groove and felt my face turn back to its normal shade. I started telling the story about Gallows Hill as I remembered it, and he'd stop me once in a while to ask, "How did that make you feel?" and give me some key describing words to help. He asked me questions about our other tours and the other evidence and EVP's that I sent in for our audition video. After about 20 minutes of storytelling intermixed with the make-up woman powdering my face to stop me from looking sweaty, he gave me some sentences that he wanted me to repeat a few times in different tones:

"It's really creepy."

"I'm starting to get really scared."

"And then we shut it down."

"Shut what down?" I asked.

"The evening. The investigation. Whatever." He replied.

"I just don't want it to sound like we shut down our business. We are absolutely still doing tours and I really hope that this television show brings us more clients. I don't really want to say that."

"Oh, no, that's not what I meant." he said.

"Okay so I'd rather not say that phrase out of context if you don't mind." I said.

He was very nice and understanding, and let me skip that one.

After the main interview, and the repeating of different phrases, he told me to stare at a piece of blue tape across the room and stay perfectly still so they could get some camera shots of me at different angles. As the cameras started slowly swiveling around my body and up above, I was trying to fight off the giggles. I don't know why, but I thought it was so funny to sit there quietly staring at a piece of masking tape on the back of a chair while all these camera lenses were making buzzing noises as they zoomed in and out at my face. It took everything in me not to bust out laughing.

And then it was over. Jason shook my hand to thank me and Corey walked in to take my place. I asked if it was okay to stay and take a few photos. He told me that of course it was okay, and asked if we wanted him to take a photo of the two of us together. Then we asked another producer to take a shot of the three of us with one of the cameras in the foreground. The staff there was really, really nice.

I set off down the hall with the same assistant producer who walked me down to the studio, to head back to the green room to wait for Corey. Since my interview was over, my appetite returned and I snacked on delicious food until she returned. We rode back to the hotel, talking about our interview experience and how many describing words they wanted us to use about being scared when, as paranormal investigators, we were usually much more excited than afraid. But we realize it's for television and that's what sells. We were a little worried about how our story would be portrayed.

Two weeks later, A&E sent a cameraman to film reenactments of our story. We were told that they had decided it would be an easier flowing storyline if we combined our bachelorette party story with our Gallows Hill story as if it happened in one evening on Gallows Hill. That was fine with me. I didn't think it really mattered when and where the stories happened.

We met our cameraman, Larry, at our office to begin filming. He had a list of different shots he needed to film. First, he wanted us to walk him around town so he could get general shots of downtown Salem. A sign that said, "Welcome to Salem," the witchy logo on the side of a police car, the cemetery, a walk down Essex Street, etc. Then we arrived back at our office to do a reenactment of seeing this apparition behind us in the photo on our computer. He told us to sit at our desk, pull up the photo, and then look at the photo, and then look at each other with a surprised expression. Do you know how hard it is to not laugh when you suddenly move your head to stare at your friend with your eyes wide? It took us many takes to get that right.

Then we were off to Gallows Hill. Many of our friends were eager to help with filming and be our extras, acting as tourists and bachelorette partygoers, so we met them in the parking lot. Larry spent a bit of time just getting dark camera shots of the path and the woods. And then it was time to walk up the path with EMF detectors and cameras in hand. This was a lot of fun. It was like being in a play, but on location. So I guess you could say it was like being in a movie but I have no idea what that actually feels like. Either way, me = movie star.

We spent eight hours that evening on Gallows Hill, walking through the woods, pushing swings, doing mock investigations while sitting on the ground, and taking pretend photos.

When the episode aired, we thought they did an amazing job. (Despite my double chin and attempts to hide my pregnancy.) Hours of filming for our nine minutes of fame. I developed a deep appreciation for all that goes into producing television and movies. Those nine minutes created a lot of buzz about my little company. We soon had many people visiting our website and commenting on social media that they saw us on *My Ghost Story*. One night, a woman even asked me for my autograph. So funny.

Our tours picked up and we became very busy. However, at this time Corey moved on to a new job as I was moving further along in my pregnancy. I enlisted the help of my husband for a while when it was just too hard to stay up so late and walk and stand for such long distances. (He was such a skeptic before. He became a believer after that!) I needed to hire more tour guides, so after many days of interviewing, I hired an amazing team who made it through the summer. It was a really tough time, though. I wasn't prepared for the growth. When I was in labor with my daughter at the end of September, I was still making phone calls and scheduling tours between contractions.

Paranormal Studies

The doors were wide open for me. Suddenly people knew who I was and they wanted that personal experience without having to join a paranormal team. My EVP's of the Lyceum were used on a show called *Haunted History* on the History Channel. I was interviewed for a public access/YouTube show called Hangin' with Harrison in the Charter Street Cemetery. Harrison was an awesome 11 year old kid with a huge following, and that opened doors to doing daytime investigations for a much younger crowd. I also started teaching "Ghost Hunting 101" inside the old firehouse building during the off season, when it was too cold to venture outside for a walking tour. Teaching was where my heart was.

My Ghost Hunting 101 included a lot of history about ghost hunting and where the field is headed. I would explain that this is not a new field, and that the public's perception of it has changed just in the last few years, mostly due to the popularity of ghost shows on TV. Just to point out how far back this goes, it is documented that a man named Athenodoros rented a house to investigate for spirits as far back as 7 A.D. Many very famous reputable people in time have considered the mystery of what happens after you die as something of great importance. For instance, Thomas Edison attempted to invent a device that could talk to the dead in 1920.

Paranormal investigation has become a very researched field

in the last couple decades. Scientific and technical-based paranormal teams use various ghost hunting equipment, of course, but they're also always looking for new equipment that might work better than the standard EMF detector or digital recorder that they're already using. And metaphysical teams are using their own intuition, research, and mystical tools. With so many people out there searching for answers right now it's very exciting!

Debunking was one of the most important subjects that I taught in my class. So many people would send me spooky photos that they had taken around Salem during a visit. They wanted me to say, "Holy cow! You caught a ghost!" They wanted validation, but I couldn't do that unless I was there. I think it's best to be 75% skeptic and 25% believer when it comes to the paranormal. You want to always try to debunk first and attempt to explain away any normal explanation before jumping to conclusions. Let me give you an example: On an investigation of a private house once, I took a photo of what looks like the apparition of a man through a sliding glass door. I was really excited at first, because seeing an apparition of a man was the major claim of the homeowners. Instead of rushing over to show them, I did everything I could to disprove what I was seeing in the photo. Turns out, the apparition in my photo was a reflection in the glass. Yeah, I know. Bummer. But sometimes it turns out that you can't debunk a photo. This makes the evidence so much more intriguing, like the photo of the man behind Corey and me on Gallows Hill. Because we did everything we could to debunk it first, it's my very favorite piece of evidence of a ghostly visitor.

Another thing to consider is debunking EVPs. There are 3 classes of EVP's. A Class A EVP is a very clear voice. Anyone and everyone can listen to that audio and everyone is in agreement as to what it says. A Class B EVP is vocal but not clear. Maybe you hear, "I'm a fake!" and someone else hears, "I love cake!" Lastly, a Class C EVP is not vocal at all, just knocks, bangs, or other noises. Again, pay careful attention to the noises that you make during recording.

After teaching Ghost Hunting 101 for quite a few months, North Shore Community College hired me to teach a class called "Paranormal Studies." I couldn't believe that people would actually pay money to take college classes about the paranormal. Times were changing! Paranormal Studies was a 6-week series and I ended up teaching it multiple times. Classes included history, theory, equipment, forming a team, plus the business paperwork to do that, an investigation of the old firehouse, and evaluation and sound editing. I remember one student asked if there was a book or something similar that talked about what each religion or culture believed about ghosts and the paranormal. I said that I didn't know and I still haven't found any reference like that. Perhaps that'll be my next book!

The House Of The Seven Gables And Old Sturbridge Village

After hearing about my community college class, I was asked to give a lecture about the paranormal at The House of the Seven Gables, a Salem landmark made famous by Nathaniel Hawthorne's novel of the same name. They would advertise it, all I had to do was show up. The lecture would explore the paranormal side of Salem's history and share my spooky findings, and then hopefully find some more by concluding the evening with an investigation. The House of the Seven Gables was a place I had always wanted to investigate, and I thought it was very validating that they had asked me. I was a little nervous speaking in front of about 50 people in a much different setting than a tour or my classroom. I had a podium with a microphone and everything. But the evening went fantastic, even though we didn't find much evidence that it was haunted—I still feel like it is though!

Next I received a phone call from a woman named Nancy at Old Sturbridge Village. She wanted to hire me to do a lecture and ghost hunt in their supposedly haunted theatre, in memory of her grandmother who used to work there. They asked if I could also bring a psychic from my paranormal team and add in some extra metaphysical teachings. I loved that idea, and asked my friend Holly to join me. We met one evening over wine and came up with a cohesive plan for our speeches and how the evening would flow.

Sturbridge is almost a two-hour drive from Salem, so we decided to leave three hours before we were supposed to be at the event, just to be safe. We packed up our gear, fliers, and business cards, and headed out in the late afternoon. When I drove on to the highway, it was at a dead standstill. We inched along as the minutes ticked by. We were so worried we were going to be late for our own event. Holly sat in the passenger seat with her eyes closed saying that she was sending out positive energy for our drive. She said she was going to keep imagining the cars parting, with all traffic lights green, and imagining us walking into the event with plenty of time to spare, manifesting our early arrival. I needed to learn more about these visualization techniques, because I was freaking out. My heart was pounding. I was so worried about seeming unprofessional.

We made it to Old Sturbridge Village at exactly the time our lecture was supposed to start. We had no set up time, and no time to calm down and focus before we began speaking. We walked on stage to an audience of around 100 people and we smiled and disguised our adrenaline and anxiety. I spoke first while Holly laid all of equipment on the table behind me so that I could talk about it later. I don't think anyone in the audience felt our tension or knew that we were late. After my usual "Ghost Hunting 101" speech, Holly added great information about using your own intuition to connect with the other side. And then it was time to turn the lights off and investigate. Our audience was excited yet somewhat apprehensive about the prospect of searching for ghosts in a haunted theatre. We passed around as much equipment as we had, dispersing what we could amongst groups of families to share. This was unlike any investigation that I had done before. It reminded me of when I used to watch

Kimberly Bizjak

Crossing Over with John Edward. It was as if each person in that theatre was having their own personal spirit experience, but with a family member and not a resident ghost of Old Sturbridge Village. Someone would raise their hand and say, "I asked my grandmother if she was here and my dowsing rods moved." Someone else would say, "I feel like it is my brother who is lighting up this KII meter!" The entire investigation was a big family reunion for those in spirit. It was a very special evening, and I can't help but think Nancy's grandmother had something to do with that.

Becoming "Psychic"

After the evening at Old Sturbridge Village, I wanted to learn even more about using my intuition. Jen and Holly were offering an introductory course in Tarot in their Salem shop. It was amazing. I learned techniques for meditating, grounding, and then how to read cards. They had a few other psychic friends join them for the class so that when it was time to read, we would each be paired up with someone who had experience with tarot and could help if we got stuck. The woman I was paired up with told me that the reading I gave her was strikingly accurate and that I had a gift. I assumed she told everyone they were a gifted psychic.

I honestly do not like the word "psychic". Hollywood has had the biggest hand in ruining it, but regular ol' mean-spirited people ruin it too. You see websites offering up "psychic services" all the time, like:

"I will improve your luck for any job"

"I will cast a spell to make you more attractive"

"I will place a powerful hex curse on your enemy"

"I will bring your love back to you"

"I will accurately predict your time of death"

These are low energy services that attract low energy clients. There was a woman in Salem who was scamming people out of thousands of dollars, saying she could remove curses. She was basically scaring sad lonely people into believing there was something wrong with them and that she— and only she — could fix it. Bad apples like that woman give psychics a bad reputation. And I'm not saying that she absolutely isn't a gifted psychic. She might be, but she's channeling the lower energies that I stay away from.

So am I psychic? I prefer to say I'm intuitive. And guess what? Everyone is! Some people are born naturally intuitive, and some people have to practice and hone their skills. It's like singing or playing a musical instrument. Some people are born with a beautiful singing voice, and some people are born with a passion for music, take lessons, work very hard, and become absolutely fantastic musical performers.

It's really not hard to predict the future. Say I pull a tarot card for you, and I pick up on a "vibe" that you're being a lazy jerk at work. To say you're going to be fired soon isn't so much about being psychic, it's using common sense and my sixth sense at the same time. And you have complete free-will to stop being a lazy jerk, or even quit before you're fired. So my prediction might be wrong after all.

When choosing an intuitive, healer, or medium, make sure you choose someone who is channeling the most positive energies for your highest good. They're doing it out of love, not fear. A healer should teach you how to best heal yourself. An intuitive should help you to better understand your own intuition. And a medium should only channel your loved ones who have the most positive amazing messages for you. I strive to be that person. My hope is that someday we can take back the word "psychic" as a positive, wonderful thing. Until then... intuitive it is!

I started searching for other ways to strengthen my intuition, and was reminded of my long forgotten love of these techniques from when I was a kid. And the more I opened my third eye, the more "paranormal" things would happen. Jen and Holly hosted a very informal girls' Tarot Night Out at a local restaurant. During an evening of laughing and drinking wine, I was gifted my own set of tarot cards. One of the women who attended had an extra set that she barely ever used. When I saw them I fell in love. She told me that that is how tarot works. You don't buy cards, cards find you. She said they belonged to me.

I started doing free tarot readings for friends and attempting to meditate more, and my ghost hunting tours became more intuitive. I'd sense more and could feel the energy change, and I would know whether an EMF detector would light up before it did. I would see spirits when I wasn't in "ghost hunter mode." I'd be driving down the street and see someone standing in the cemetery. One instance as that happened, I glanced over again, and he was gone. One day I was walking down the street, glancing at my cell phone, and saw a man with a black bowler hat walking toward me. Right as he was close enough to pass me, I looked up to see him straight on, and he vanished.

Letting The Spirits Go

One evening while taking a tour group down to the basement of the firehouse, we were attempting to contact our usual resident spirit of a little girl, and I could feel her sadness. I felt like I wanted to cry. I finished the tour that night and sat alone in my office thinking about her. My tours were so busy and going so well that I rarely stopped to think about the spirits. Why they are here and why they haven't crossed over. When I was only speaking to them through paranormal equipment, there was a disconnect, but using my intuition was different, and I couldn't ignore it anymore— I had to do something. It had been months since that brick was thrown across the room, but there was still negative energy to clear.

I invited Jen and Holly to spend an evening with me in the firehouse to cleanse and connect. They sat on opposite ends of the room, each with a notepad, and began to sketch what they saw and felt in the space. When we came together in the middle of the room, both sketches looked almost identical. It was a farm house with a pond. I had never told Jen and Holly about the rumors of the little girl who once lived on Bridget Bishop's land. And I know I said before that I thought she haunted the Lyceum and the Firehouse. Who's to say that her land didn't used to cover both areas, as they are right across the narrow street from each other. We came to the conclusion that she's probably just trying to contact anyone who would listen.

We drew a 5-pointed star on the floor with a circle around it in salt. Contrary to popular belief, a pentacle is not a symbol of evil. The top point of the star represents yourself or your spirit. The other 4 points represent earth, air, fire, and water. The outside circle represents the circle of life and never-ending cycle of energy. It has received a bad reputation mostly from Hollywood, but also from certain religions intent on discrediting pagan symbols from long ago. It's usually seen drawn on the floor or a wall in horror movies, sometimes even written in blood. It is not a satanic symbol. We drew a pentacle on the ground to call upon the forces of Mother Nature to help protect us. Earth for grounding, water for intuition, air for intellect, and fire for passion. Covering the circle with salt is another cleansing element, representing the sea and the waves washing in and pulling negative energy away with it. We called to this girl whose name we believe was Isabelle. We told her it was time to move on and be with her family. Jen and Holly believed she had a brother waiting for her on the other side. We sent her love.

Next, we lit sage and put it in a seashell and began to walk around the basement moving the smoke with a feather: sage representing earth, the smoke was our fire, the shell representing water, and the feather representing air. We set our intention to cleanse this space of any negative entity and energy, and returned to our circle to cleanse our own energy before closing our ritual. The little girl's spirit moved on. Did she have something to do with the spirit who threw that brick? I'm not entirely sure— but I *did* know that we no longer had resident ghosts in the firehouse. Any spirit who came through on our tours after that was a family member of a tourist.

Goodbye

I started feeling like I didn't belong in Salem anymore. It felt like it was time to move on. Truth be told, owning a business there was not easy. It's a little bit like the energy of 1692 still lingers. If you are an outsider and you are showing signs of success, you start feeling as if you're being hunted. When I first started, another business started advertising a paranormal investigation tour using very close to the same name as my business. I sent him a cease and desist order from a lawyer—*Don't mess with me.* And then the City of Salem passed an ordinance saying that tours had to end by 11pm. My tours ended at midnight, sometimes later in October. I had to go to numerous city council meetings to plead my case and explain that my tourists were not a rowdy crowd, but a very quiet small group capped at 20 people. After a lot of stress and many meetings, I was able to get a variance for my company. Also, in addition to a tour guide license that you are required to obtain by taking a test on the history of Salem, if you are doing any type of psychic work, you need an extra license for that, and they only hand out so many of those per year as to not saturate the tourism market. (Really, you even need a permit in Salem to hold a garage sale!) So because it was feeling like I was moving toward the intuitive side of talking to the dead, Salem wasn't where I would be welcome to do that. Also, we had a new baby and our family in Seattle was missing us. It was time to head back home. Finally, regrettably, inevitably, I sold my company, and drove across the country in 2013, saying goodbye to my beloved second home.

THREE

◆ ◆ ◆

Air

Merchant's Cafe

When we first moved back to Seattle, it felt great to be home. I really missed all of my friends and family, and I loved that our kids were able to regularly see their grandparents, aunts, uncles, and cousins. We moved into a cute old quirky house that the neighborhood had nicknamed "The Witch House" because it had pointed peaks and round windows. Seemed a fitting place to call home after living in the Witch City. As wonderful as it was to be home, I deeply missed Salem. I missed the seasons: The fall colors, the snow, the warm summer beaches. Most of all, I missed my witchy circle of friends and nights filled with wine, laughter, tarot and pendulums. My old friends in Seattle were great, but I needed a new circle here. I joined a group on meetup called "Mystic Mamas" and found my tribe. These women had the same energy as my friends in Salem. They were all immensely helpful and I began to learn so much from each of them. We would hold circle around a fire pit and dance, meditate, and exchange words and energy; and listen to fascinating presentations from guest speakers on all sorts of metaphysical subjects. Seattle started to feel more like home than it did before I left.

After a few months of settling in, I began working a part-time "non woo-woo" job, and I was really missing spirit. My friend Megan invited me to go to Seattle's Underground Tour with her, which was something I hadn't done since I was a kid. Apparently there was a restaurant called Merchant's Café in Pioneer Square that has a haunted history, that Megan heard about on a show called *Dead Files*. She suggested that we stop by there for lunch after the Underground Tour.

During lunch, we met with Darcy, the cafe's owner, and Megan told her that she had seen her episode on TV. She was so friendly and talkative about her experiences. She went behind the counter and grabbed an entire binder where she kept photos and entries of paranormal evidence about the restaurant. We chatted on and off while she waited on other tables. I told Darcy about my tour company and how I was on *My Ghost Story,* and we laughed about the ridiculousness of filming a television show and how long the process takes. She told me that I should teach a class in the room downstairs and that we could run a Groupon for it and split the profits. I loved that idea. I would be back in my groove and bring a little bit of Salem magick to Seattle.

So I purchased some ghost hunting equipment (I had sold all of mine with the sale of my business) and started teaching a Ghost Hunting 101 class at Merchant's Café. Merchant's Café is Seattle's oldest restaurant. Built in 1890, (so super new compared to Salem) it has always been a restaurant, but once held a speakeasy and a gambling room. The hotel above used to be one of Seattle's most infamous brothels. The basement is actually a portion of Underground Seattle, with brick arches that used to be windows that looked onto the street.

The paranormal claims include seeing a man in the main restaurant who is thought to be an old employee named Otto who haunts the building—but he's actually a nice guy who helps out. He's been known to turn off the televisions when asked to at the end of the evening. There's also the apparition of a woman who has been seen downstairs, and shadows of two children who haunt the basement rumored to have died in the Great Seattle Fire. (I found no evidence of any deaths at all during the Great Seattle Fire.) There are also the usual "haunted location" knocks, creaks, slamming doors, faucets turning on and off by themselves, and objects moving on their own.

Some evenings at Merchant's Café were pretty slow in paranormal activity, and some had interesting KII hits, and revealed great EVP's. I would catch a male voice on occasion, and sometimes a child's voice. We could never quite make out what they were saying. Some of my attendees captured strange photos of shadowy anomalies, and some would swear they saw figures inside the caged-off bar area at the end of the room. It was a great experience to spend time there each week, but I ultimately decided to discontinue the class. The loud bar upstairs wasn't a conducive environment for a quiet ghost hunt. And the only restrooms in the building were in the basement— which meant that intoxicated, loud patrons would hobble down the already slanted old stairwell and see us at the bottom and start asking questions about what we were doing. Additionally, the kitchen was just on the other side of a curtain from our investigation, which was also loud.

Around the time I was thinking about discontinuing the Groupon deal, my stepmom passed away after a fifteen-year battle with cancer. After that, talking about the dead wasn't fun anymore, so my decision to quit teaching the class was solidified. The death of a close family member gave me a completely different perspective though, and all of a sudden put me in a "club" with others who have been through a loss. It was nice to feel like I could help, and in turn, it helped me.

Signs From Spirit

After teaching Ghost Hunting at Merchant's Café, and while attending circles and events with the Mystic Mamas group, I began taking any and all metaphysical workshops offered at an amazing holistic space called Intra-Space: Energy medicine, Intuitive Development, Sound Baths, Psychic Panels, etc. All the hippie shit I could find! I realized it was actually really amazing NOT being in Salem anymore. In Seattle this information was shared widely and not kept a secret, in fear someone would start a business exactly like yours. As I said, the energy of 1692 still lingers there. It feels the same as keeping healing a secret in fear of being hanged. I was in the hippie free-loving Pacific Northwest again! I could give tarot readings wherever to whoever I wanted! I also resurrected my Ghost Hunting class at IntraSpace, but called it "A Spirited Evening Connecting with the Other Side."

I was also busy reading every book I could find about mediumship and psychic abilities. Authors such as Carolyn Myss, Sonya Chochette, James Van Praagh, Gordon Smith, and Theresa Caputo.

Eryn, my friend who led the Mystic Mamas group, is an amazing intuitive Shaman. She watched *My Ghost Story* when it popped up on Facebook one day, and emailed me this whole explanation (*She called it a "download"?*) of why she felt I was meant to live in Salem. She said that in a past life, (*Do I even believe in past lives?*) I knew one of the accused witches in 1692, and although I wasn't hanged myself, I felt like I couldn't do anything about it and watched helplessly. She told me that I am meant to be a healer in this lifetime. She introduced me to her friend Sarah, who has a gift for seeing energy, and I had an energy session and reading with her. She told me that I am a medium and that if I didn't start embracing it, I'd start getting whacked on the head by spirits until I started to. *(She's right, by the way! Heed that advice!)* She urged that if I was open to it, and asked my guides for help (*I have guides?!*), I would be amazing at it. I also visited a medium and a tarot reader at an Intuitive Fair, and they both also told me I was a medium and a healer. Okay, okay, I got it, Universe. Thanks.

Next, I came across an article that stated reiki helps a lot with mediumship. So because energy is energy, spirit energy, energy in your body, energy in a plant— it's all the same. I decided to become a Reiki Master and to help connect my interests and gifts.

Here is where I should probably also mention that I am a Licensed Massage Therapist. I became licensed back in 2001 so I could work part-time for full-time pay as I put myself through college, and I continued to see clients throughout the years. Becoming a Reiki Master would give me the continuing education credits I needed to reinstate my massage license, which I was feeling a pull to do since arriving back in Washington. I remembered that one class during massage school was about energy work. A guest teacher came in to teach us how to feel the energy of someone's body. She showed us how to scan a body and pay attention to any warmth or vibration in your hands. At the time, I actually thought it was a bunch of bull. How could you feel that someone's shoulder was bothering them just by touching them? Or, actually, she said you didn't even have to touch a person to feel their energy— you could put your hands a few inches above the body and feel the same energy. I challenged this concept. I told her that I wanted to try an experiment: I would leave the room, and a student would scan a volunteer classmate by moving their hands from head to toe a few inches above them as they lay down. Someone would write down all the places in the body where they felt something, and then I would come back in and see if I felt the energy in the same places.

I left the room for a bit and came back in to do my scan. Every single place she had stopped, I stopped. I was shocked. It was amazing that we each felt a sensation in our hands in the same places of the body. During my years as a massage therapist, I would feel the energy of each client and know exactly what areas needed to be worked on, and where in the body the pain referred. I would also feel the energy of their whole aura; their vibe, their personality. Massage therapy is wonderful for healing physical ailments, and, of course, for relaxation. But more importantly, it provides deep emotional and mental therapy. Over the years, I learned that people would open up to me, tell me their problems, and I would offer advice. I would concentrate on helping them release and let go of energy that isn't for their highest good. There is deep emotional and physical release and healing during many of my sessions. As I was awakening to the notion that I was doing my own form of energy healing all along, I loved knowing that I was making a major difference in my client's day-to-day lives. I was excited to learn more about this energy and receive my certification in Reiki.

Reiki

I drove down to Portland, Oregon to take Reiki 1 and 2 over an entire weekend. There were six of us in our instructor's cozy home. We learned the history of reiki, reiki symbols, and then we were attuned to reiki energy. Here is a peek into my journal that day:

I just finished a meditation to receive my Reiki I attunement. Our instructor and Reiki Master came over to lay her hands on my shoulders, and it was like a warm tingly energy washing over me. She had me put my hands above my head in prayer form, and the energy was so strong I felt dizzy. I had to open my eyes slightly to center myself. When she came around to the front of me and opened my hands to tap and blow, it felt tingly all the way from my head to my feet.

The Reiki II attunement wasn't nearly as exciting. However, I was distracted. There was a guy in class who had a tickle in his throat during the first part of the meditation, and he kept coughing. I was concentrating on sending reiki energy to his throat to soothe his cough. As soon as I started doing that, he stopped coughing. We all talked about our experience of the attunement afterward, and I said that I was spending the first bit trying to help my classmate. I guess I was surprised that no one else in the room thought to do this. Aren't we all healers here? Not even our instructor and Reiki Master thought to pause the meditation and heal? It seemed like an amazing opportunity to help someone and also make it a teaching moment.

We used teddy bears to practice distance healing. We partnered up and gave each other only the name and city of a friend or family member. We were supposed to send reiki to the bear and see if we picked up on ailments from this person we know nothing about. I intuitively picked up on something "off" about the left shoulder and right leg. I was picturing what this person looked like and imagined they were in a motorcycle or bicycle accident. I also stopped at the head because I felt this person needed focus and direction. Turns out this was my partner's teenage son. And he did indeed have issues with chronic pain in his left shoulder and right knee. It wasn't due to an accident, however. It was due to military boot camp training. She got weepy and thanked me when I told her I attempted to give him clarity and focus for his future. She said he really needed that. I was very surprised that every single person in that room was dead on about their intuitive findings.

Even though I feel like I've used reiki since massage school, I was told that this energy is different from the energy I feel everyday. This still confuses me and I disagree. After Reiki I, I spent hours that evening lying in bed researching different types of energy on my phone. I found a great metaphor: There are different types of water— all are water but not the same. Water from a mountain stream is not the same as water in a puddle, or a lake, or the ocean. It's all made up of the same thing, but they're all very different. The water metaphor stuck with me. Even when I practiced Reiki I visualize it as flowing like water. My partner that day even told me that it felt like water when I channeled it. Maybe this has something to do with my watery Pisces energy.

I have been told that perhaps you're attuned to reiki energy in a past life. After being a Reiki Master for quite a few years now, I believe that all energy is the same. This may be an unpopular opinion to some, but I believe that that's mostly due to human ego, and maybe each type of modality wants to feel special, maybe. There's different titles, different symbols. But energy is energy.

But what exactly is it? There are names all over the world for universal life force energy. In Japan it is called Reiki. In China it is called Chi. In Sanskrit it is called Prana. Some call it spirit. Some call it vibes that surround you, or individually it is your Aura.

Meridians are a Chinese medicine concept relating to how chi flows through the body, by paths, channels, and energy healing roads. Yin and yang, female and male sides of the body. This is how Acupuncture points work. It's amazing where acupuncturists put needles that seemingly are nowhere near where your pain is, and it subsides.

Reiki is a little bit like acupuncture in that way to the Japanese. It clears blockages, according to the way your life force energy flows through your body. You channel it with your hands. The way I was taught reiki was that it is a very strict modality. The history is magical and tells us that Usui climbed high atop a mountain, and after many days of searching and fasting, was given this energy from the gods. He was attuned to this special reiki energy. It was a gift and he began healing. As I said, I honestly think that an attunement is not necessary and that everyone has this ability with practice and positive intention.

Try it for yourself. Feel the energy of another person's body. It could feel cold, hot, tingly. It might feel like there's a slight gravitational pull. Practice with your own hands. Put both palms together and slowly separate your hands until you're making an imaginary ball in your hands. Can you feel it? Bring your hands closer, and then farther apart. You can feel this energy. You can feel your aura, your vibes, your reiki, your chi, your prana. You can even try it with a friend and close your eyes and throw your ball of energy to each other. See if you can feel where your partner was aiming.

Try what I tried in massage school many years ago. See if you can feel where someone is having physical issues in their body. I started with this simple experiment and can now tell someone what emotional reasons correlate with their physical pain. I don't have to touch a person now. I can do it just by looking at you. I can read someone's energy over the phone now.

I also want you to practice sensing where in the body did you *feel* something when you imagine different things. Picture in your mind: your significant other, your child, your beloved pet. And then imagine a spider, a dark alleyway, a monster. Feel it in your body. Where does that feeling come from? What does that tell you?

The Chakras

Your aura and the seven main energy centers of your body (called Chakras) change day by day, hour by hour. Front to back, back to front. The word chakra is Sanskrit for "wheel." So when someone says, "What color is my aura?", it is probably many colors, and those colors change constantly. I feel that I have a unique deep connection to chakra healing work. Everything in the body— physical, mental, and spiritual — makes sense to me if you connect it with a chakra.

You have more than 7 chakras but the following are the main ones:

Our first chakra is called the Root Chakra. The mantra is "I am." Its color is red. It is located in the lowest part of your torso, at the base of your spine. It represents earth, and grounding. This is where issues with safety, finances, weight, home life, stability, childhood, survival, tribe, and family come up. This is your stability and your foundation in life. Without roots, a tree will die. Our root chakra governs our Bones (our scaffolding), legs, ankles, knees, and adrenals.

When I was first learning the chakra system as a massage therapist, I would be sitting quietly at the end of the massage table, holding acupressure points on my client's feet when suddenly I would feel the presence of a spirit in the room, and would receive messages from my client's family members. At the time,

I didn't want to seem crazy so I didn't relay these messages. My clients were seeing me for a therapeutic massage, not messages from loved ones on the other side. Also, I thought, "Why am I getting these messages when I'm touching someone's feet? That's so weird!" Now I understand that it is because our feet are connected to our root chakra and the root is the energy of our family and ancestors. When I see clients for mediumship sessions now, I concentrate on their root chakra.

Root Chakra Mantras:

I am grounded.

I am safe.

I am centered.

I am comfortable in my own body.

I am independent.

Our second chakra is called the Sacral Chakra: The mantra is "I feel." Its color is orange. It is located in the lower abdomen, just below the navel. It represents water. This is where issues with gut feelings, literal creativity, change, polarity, movement, pleasure, sexuality, sensuality, desire, relationships, and being overly emotional come up. It governs our kidneys, bladder, genitals, and lower back.

Lack of creativity and gut instinct are the main issues that arise when working with my client's sacral chakras. Many people believe that their intuition comes from their Third Eye but that is a completely different type of intuition. Your gut intuition, when you "just know" something deep down is a feeling that comes from your sacral chakra. Knowing how to feel this intuition in your own body is a really important first step in intuitive development.

Sacral Chakra Mantras:

I feel creative.

I feel pleasure.

I feel my intuition.

I feel desirable.

I feel my emotions.

Our third chakra is called the Solar Plexus Chakra: The mantra is "I do." Its color is yellow. It is located at your sternum in the center of your rib cage. It represents fire. Power, will, energy, metabolism, transformation, self esteem, and assertiveness. Think of the color yellow as the sun burning bright. It governs muscles, digestion (gallbladder, stomach, intestines), and sight. It burns and breaks things down (digestion, muscles).

The solar plexus is the core of our life source energy (or Chi.) Will power and self esteem are the main issues that come up for my clients in their Solar Plexus. Self confidence is a difficult issue to help someone with, but breaking down and burning personal fears is the best first step when beginning Solar Plexus energy work.

Solar Plexus Mantras:

I do have willpower.

I do shine bright.

I do transform.

I do have strength.

I do assert energy.

Our fourth chakra is called the Heart Chakra. The mantra is "I love." Its color is green. It is located at your heart center. It represents the element of air. This is where you love, have compassion for all things, and give and receive. This is also unselfish, universal love, and any healing that you do for anyone else. Anything unselfish is heart energy. The heart chakra is our first higher chakra. The lower four are strictly in and for our bodies. The fourth chakra is where we start connecting with energy higher than our physical selves. The heart chakra governs the heart, lungs, arms, hands, blood pressure, and touch.

Think in terms of the intentions of gift giving. For instance, giving a gift from the heart versus the solar plexus. A gift from the heart would be out of love, but a gift from the solar plexus would be out of power. A gift from the root chakra would be for bonding, perhaps a family heirloom. Giving and receiving is the most common issue when working with my clients over the years. People tend to give too much and have a hard time receiving.

Heart Chakra Mantras:

I love myself.

I love others.

I love the Earth.

I love to give.

I love to receive.

Our fifth chakra is called the Throat Chakra. The mantra is "I speak." Its color is blue. It is located in the center of the neck. The element is ether. This is where we express truth, communicate, express emotional creativity, manifest what we desire.speaking, and hearing. It governs the ears, throat, teeth, thyroid, shoulders.

The issue that arises most with throat chakra energy is speaking what you feel and letting go of worrying what others think of you. Singing and sound healing works really well to balance your throat chakra. Creative writing and poetry is wonderfully healing as well.

Throat Chakra Mantras:

I speak my truth.

I speak love.

I speak creativity.

I speak as I sing.

I speak as I write.

Our sixth chakra is our Third Eye Chakra. The mantra is "I see." Its color is indigo or clear. It is located above your eyes in the center of your forehead. The element is light. This is where intuition, imagination, visioning, and expressing what you want happens. It is our command center, our way to see forward, achieve goals and wisdom.   It governs the brain, eyes, pineal gland, base of the skull, and our brow (headaches, vision problems, nightmares).

To practice opening your third eye, the best thing to do is stop your ego brain. Clear and become open. In order to see, you have to stop being in the picture. It's a misconception that our gut feelings come from here. That's a very common theme that comes up in my sessions. Your gut feelings come from your sacral chakra, in your body. Foresight is third eye energy. Seeing signs and understanding which direction to turn for your highest good, and making goals to get there.

Third Eye Mantras:

I see forward.

I see my goals.

I see my imagination.

I see my wisdom.

I see my light.

Our seventh chakra is the Crown Chakra. The mantra is "I understand" or "I know." Its color is typically violet, although sometimes it is portrayed as white or gold. It is located in the space directly above your head. There is no element associated with it. It is the void. This is your spirituality and connection. It is limitless, pure, spirit. It is manifestation, and service. It governs the central nervous system, skin, pituitary, energetic body, and mental body. When you are experiencing depression or exhaustion, it is typically a crown chakra issue.

The crown chakra is your personal spiritual connection to something bigger than yourself. Call it God, The Universe, or Higher Energy, etc, whatever resonates with you. This energy is knowing that you aren't alone in this life and there is a bigger purpose.

Crown Chakra Mantras:

I know spirituality.

I know connection.

Ghost Stories & Hippie Sh*t

I know service.

I know I am guided.

I know I am limitless.

The following is my chakra balancing meditation for grounding, for opening up, and letting go:

"I want you to find a comfortable place to do this meditation where you won't be disturbed. You can lie down on your back, or sit in a chair with your palms up on your lap. And when you get comfortable, I want you to take three deep breaths, in through your nose, and out through your mouth.

Breathe.

I want you to think about— focus your attention on— the area right above your head. This is your crown chakra. There is energy there. I want you to imagine a beautiful white light that is flowing and spinning and is just right above your head. It's connecting you to a higher source. The Universe, God, Mother Nature, whatever speaks to you, but this is a space that is bigger than yourself. And as you're watching this white light spin, I want you to imagine compassion and harmony and peace. I want you to let go of any feeling of depression or exhaustion, and bring in this connection to spirituality and manifestation. Spirit energy.

Next I want you to imagine the space on your forehead, right above and between your eyes where your third eye lives. I want you to imagine a beautiful purple spinning energy light circling here. While you imagine this light, I want you to imagine that this light is bringing you intuition and imagination and vision. When this light spins correctly and brightly, you can achieve your goals. This is where you see signs from the universe and your future. This is where wisdom comes from. I want you to let go of your ego. I want you to see without you being in the picture.

Next I want you to move down to your neck and throat area. This is where your throat chakra lives. This color is a beautiful bright spinning blue light. While you are imagining this bright blue light, I want you to bring in the idea of expressing your own truth, your emotional creativity. Your sense of speaking and hearing and breathing. Just open clear communication throughout your whole being. And I want you to let go of anything opposite of expressing your own truth. I want you to let go of this feeling of *I shouldn't say that* or *what would someone think of me.*

I want you to move down to your heart chakra next. This beautiful, beautiful green light that is spinning at your chest. This *is* your love center. This is where harmony and trust, and a love for yourself and a love for others, resides. A lot of love. I want you to imagine this beautiful green light bringing you so much love, and feeling true universal, unconditional, unselfish love. This is your giving and receiving, and your compassion for all things. I want you to let go of any sense of not having a balanced heart. So if you are giving more than you are receiving, or maybe you are receiving more than you are giving, I want you to let go of this imbalance and just think of love.

Next I want you to focus on your solar plexus chakra, which is just under your chest, in the area of your sternum. Imagine a bright yellow spinning light. This is where your mental energy comes from. The wisdom of your own power, your self esteem. This is your own ability to transform your life. This is a yellow color, your fire, your sun burning bright. I want you to let go of any self criticism, self doubt, self esteem issues. A feeling of not feeling assertive, feeling of weakness. I want you to let go of all of that and know that you are powerful.

Next I want you to go down a little lower to your sacral chakra, which is about near your belly button. And you are going to imagine a bright beautiful orange light spinning there. Your sacral chakra is where your gut feelings come from. Your desire, your sexuality, your sensuality. Where your emotions and your creativity live. I want you to let go of not feeling good enough, and I want you to bring in joy.

Next is your root chakra, which is all the way down at your tailbone. The root chakra is red, a beautiful bright red spinning light. This is where I want you to feel safe and grounded and stable. I want you to let go of any issues you have ever had with your finances, your family relationships. You are safe and you are grounded and you are connected to this earth.

Now I want you to imagine that all of these chakras are all spinning perfectly the same and together.

And when you're ready, you can open your eyes."

Sound Healing

After reinstating my massage license and beginning to see clients again after becoming Reiki 1 and 2 certified, I joined my friend Krizten at Intraspace for my Reiki Master certification. A few months later, I was also guided to learn sound healing with the use of tuning forks. With my background as a sound designer, it just made sense, something else that connected my gifts.

I'm going to explain a little about Psychoacoustics: the psychological study of hearing. Sound is one of the most powerful means to affect the response of the body. Sound is so commonplace in human existence that we don't realize how important it is as a force in our emotional lives. Consider how empty a movie seems when we only see the picture without the soundtrack. Even when we hear dialog, a great deal of the emotional impact is lost without environmental sounds and underscore music. What do you do in a scary part of a movie? You cover your eyes. Try plugging your ears next time. Sound is a powerful element of experience. We enjoy sound. We enjoy manipulating sound, listening to sound, and playing games with sound. We fill time with sound. Some feel uncomfortable with lack of sound. All sensory inflow alters the balance of our emotional state, even if slightly. Sound actually directly stimulates the reward centers of the brain. Sight and hearing are both called "distance senses." All other senses— smell, taste, and touch —

only supply data of conditions in close contact with our bodies. An interconnection exists between physics and the psychology of hearing. Sounds like the blowing wind, sea waves, and birds singing are more audible sounds. They have the ability to interact with emotions and mood to affect feeling. Music is the human effort to express emotion.

If reiki is energy healing, sound is vibrational healing. You feel goosebumps when you listen to music because the vibration is opening your spine and your energy centers. Each tuning fork's tone correlates to a chakra. Our bodies are made up of 80% water, so when you are using sound as a vibration, the water in your body can sense and be affected by the vibration as energy. It can also heal by triggering and breaking up the emotions and physical ailments in your body. It can create a shift in your cells. You have energetic blocks in your chakras, and they vibrate apart when sounds permeate them. When sound travels through a medium, the medium is affected by it because our bodies have substance.

As a Massage Therapist, Tarot Reader, Reiki Master, and Certified Sound Healer, I was attracting new clients and I deeply loved my job. It was now time to strengthen my mediumship abilities further.

Through The Veil

T hirteen people sat in a circle in a small earthy room in downtown Seattle. The woman hosting the workshop took us through a variety of different meditation exercises, and then we went around the room to talk about the experience after each exercise. The first was a grounding exercise which was not new to me, but we tried three different ways to visualize: a tree trunk from your root to the core of the earth, a waterfall, and then a beam of light. I think I prefer the good old fashioned tree trunk method *(perhaps the watery Pisces in me needed earthy roots?),* but the other two were interesting. Next, we did a protection exercise where we visualized a protective bubble around us, also known as our aura. Visualize it close to you, far away, the room, the building, the whole city of Seattle, and then above you, in front of you, etc. Everyone in the room said they felt most comfortable with it about two-three feet from them, and that making it as big as Seattle was like inviting everyone's energy in, and it felt like a big cocktail party, and they didn't want to be there. They didn't feel safe. I felt completely the opposite. I liked the cocktail party. It was more fun and open. I felt claustrophobic when I brought it back in. I felt anxiety. The next exercise was to practice "being inside your head." We focused on our right toe, then our left knee, then our stomach, heart, and so on. Then we focused on the space above our heads, and then the space right outside our left ear. And then focus on our head, directly behind your eyes— That was interesting, it really gave a different sense of centeredness. Like, *"Wow, I'm here!"* Next, we focused on our chakras. We "dialed down" our lower chakras and "dialed up" our higher ones, which help with spirit communication.

Next we had to tune in and do all of these things at the same time. It reminded me of "Chi Running": hips forward, ankles relaxed, crown high, lean forward. This was: stay grounded, be in your head, upper chakras open, aura where you feel protected. Doing all of this at once was a strange sensation, especially when I hadn't decided whether to bring my protective energy bubble in like everyone else or go to a cocktail party. I opted for the cocktail party. If I wanted to embrace my mediumship abilities, that seemed to make the most sense—invite some people in.

While doing all of these exercises in sync, we were told to visualize a relative or friend who has passed on, sitting in a chair in front of us. I decided the obvious choice was to picture my stepmom. I tried and tried to invite her to sit in my imaginary chair, and I could eventually see her there, kind of fuzzy or blurry, but smiling. All of a sudden I got this overwhelming feeling of sadness. I mean, really. Tears started coming to my eyes and I pictured my dad's face. I thought, *"Holy crap. This is what mediumship truly is. She's telling me she's worried about my dad through a feeling."* Then all of a sudden my father-in-law was sitting in my chair, much clearer than my mom. He was beaming, and it was like he was saying, *"Hey! How are you!?"* And then I got this really strong feeling of love as I pictured my son and my daughter. *"Aww, he's sending his love to his grandchildren."* I thought.

After that, it got extra weird, and this woman who I've never seen before popped up in my chair. She was an older woman, maybe early 60's, with brown hair. She kept saying *"Carol, Cheryl, Carol, Cheryl."* And I thought, *"What the heck lady. Who are you? Get out of my chair! I was talking to someone!"* And then the exercise was over. We took turns talking about our experience Some people said they had conversations with grandparents, that they were reminded of childhood memories, etc. But no one was saying anything close to what I had experienced, except this older woman sitting next to me. She said that she tried talking to her mom but she wasn't speaking. She said that for whatever reason, she felt like she would be able to go around the room and touch each of us and that she might be able to communicate with each of our loved ones. A couple of people passed on sharing anything at all— and I was going to pass too, so I didn't sound like a crazy person. But because this woman told her experience, I thought I'd tell mine. I mentioned this woman that I saw, and one of the women in the room— who had passed on telling us her experience— gasped and started tearing up. She said that I described her mother Carol and that her name is Cheryl. She said her friends and family always call her and her mother the wrong name and it became a joke. This information blew me away. This mediumship stuff was getting real. Honestly, I felt like I could have left for the evening, that I could go home and process what I had learned and experienced, but it was time for one last exercise.

We tried again with instructions on speaking with the same person or someone different. This time my grandma appeared in my chair, smiling, but it was only for a second, because the instructor interjected with instructions to imagine an object that was maybe given to us by that person, so I pictured a little figurine that my other grandma had given me. I thought maybe I should be seeing her in my chair instead. Then I saw my grandfather, and then my father-in-law again.... And then everything got all crazy and swirly. This is the part of my book where people might seriously question my sanity, because at this point, I was! The only way I can describe it was that I was imagining this tornado of people popping in and out and morphing into each other. Some people I knew, some people I didn't. We were then prompted to trade healing with the person sitting in our chair, to ask them what you could do for them. I was feeling overwhelmed and had no idea what I could possibly do for all these people. Our instructor then prompted us to ask what they can do for me. What messages can they give you? How can they help you? I thought that sounded like a much better question, so I asked. All of a sudden the swirling of people began to fade as two beings made of bright white light came toward me. It was as if they each grabbed one of my arms and sat me back down in my chair. (Not that I was actually standing, but they brought me back into the room, so to speak). It was as if these beings said, *"That's enough for one day. You're done. You can practice this more on your own when you're alone." "What the heck just happened? Where those my guides that everyone tells me I have?"* I sat in awe and confusion with my eyes closed, and waited for everyone else to complete the exercise.

More Signs From Spirit

So here I was, the girl who loved to watch Ghost Hunters and became one, and now I'm watching Long Island Medium, and I'm becoming a medium. Day by day, workshop by workshop, book by book... I looked for the signs from the Universe, the Divine, the Goddess, (who or whatever is bigger than myself), and I followed them.

I started giving friends free mediumship readings. The things I said and the things I knew not only surprised my friends but surprised me as well. *How did I know these things?* I honestly had no idea and no book or teacher could accurately portray this to my left-brained mind. Although I was learning not to need the ghost hunting equipment anymore, it was still a security blanket for me. I still felt like I needed proof, no matter how many people I did readings for, who completely resonated and validated what I told them. It wasn't proof enough for me.

I started reading cards at a monthly intuitive fair, which was a much different experience and energy than reading in my home. During one reading I asked a woman if she has a really goofy, fun, crazy job, and she said she was a professional clown! *Really, I can't make this shit up.* I told another woman that she had really amazing mama bear instincts, and she showed me a tattoo of a bear on her forearm that she'd gotten for exactly that reason. I asked another woman why I felt like her dad's money was literally dirty— not like *bad* money— but caked with mud. She told me he passed away in a landslide and it pained her to think about what to do with the insurance money.. I told another woman that I saw a nursing cap and yellow lilies, and she said she's a nurse and that is her favorite flower.

Once, I was hired for a private ghost hunt by a woman in Seattle. During the hunt, I "heard" the name of a man who happened to be this woman's brother. In another investigation, I picked up a name, and the woman who lived there said that was the name of the old homeowner who had died of a heart attack in the house. She said she still gets his mail.

Another time, I said out loud that I felt a spirit's name was Irene or Irina, and when we listened back to the audio recorder, you could hear "Irina" very clearly after I said it. That was amazing and exactly the kind of proof I was looking for.

The next reading I did, I brought my ghost hunting equipment and my tarot cards, but didn't end up using them as much, if at all. The reading felt different. I just told her what I felt and saw. It was that easy. I described her uncle accurately, and then described her grandmother's backyard right down to the odd patio furniture. As I mentioned a suicide from a drug overdose and it resonated with her, an orb flew across the room for validation.

My husband and I built a healing studio detached from our home. We constructed the entire thing completely on our own. A beautiful space tucked into the hillside amongst the redwood trees with an amazing view of Puget Sound. It was

129

the perfect soothing place for seeing clients for readings, reiki, massage, and also tuning fork therapy. Each service started blending with the next. Loved ones would come through during a massage, or, for instance, I'd end up giving a tarot reading after a reiki session because I picked up something odd about a woman's arm and told her she needs to write.

So what was I learning that helped me become a medium? I feel like I was not learning anything new, but actually unlearning everything that got in the way of my own intuition along the way. I would love to teach this to you in the next section. You'll find helpful information for intuitive development intermixed with my own journal entries of personal meditation and shamanic journeying during my own spiritual pilgrimage.

FOUR

◆ ◆ ◆

Spirit

A Guide

"As I was walking down a path in the woods, one of the "light beings" from my last workshop was peeking at me from behind a tree. I was instructed to walk to a clearing and my guide would meet me in a gazebo. When I arrived, I saw a young middle eastern man. Reminded me a bit of Aladdin. He smiled and I asked his name. I heard noises in my right ear. A squeaking noise, that reminded me of what it feels like when you're underwater and your ears pop. Tin noises. Vibration. Slight ear pain. Like listening to an EVP. Maybe it was a squeaking, maybe it was a word over and over. It was hard to tell, but it was definitely coming from my physical ears. When this man spoke to me in my mind's eye, no sound came out of his mouth. I knew that this was the man whom I spent years writing back and forth to as a child, the man I knew as Yeley."

-AUGUST 16, 2016

Meditation And Mindfulness

I can't stress enough how much meditation and being mindful is important, no matter what you do in your life. You must learn to quiet your mind, let go, and ground. This doesn't need to take a lot of time and there is no right or wrong in the way you meditate. If you only have ten minutes to yourself to hide in your bathroom and center yourself while your kids watch television, then that's perfect. If you happen to have time to lie down for an hour for a more in depth meditation, even better.

Sit with your eyes closed and take at least three deep breaths. Feel your feet on the ground and imagine vines slowly wrapping around your ankles and down the bottoms of your feet. These vines are not scary. They grow down under the floor beneath your feet, down through the soil and rock beneath you. They grow straight down to the center of the earth and wrap around the core of the earth. It creates a magnetic pull, a force of gravity, holding you safe onto mother earth and connecting her to you. These vines are your roots. You are like a tree and you grow while connected here. Feel the pull. You are safe, you are grounded, you are connected. You are of this earth.

You can find ways to ground and connect with the earth daily without even taking time to meditate. Go outside and put your bare feet literally on the earth. It feels so refreshing and so centering. Put your feet in the grass, sand, or water. Putting your feet in salt water and dipping them into the ocean is the best form of grounding that I've found. The ocean calls to our inner souls. Anytime you're feeling stressed and anxious, get out of any man-made building and feel your feet in nature. Just being outside in nature is wonderful for you. Go to the woods and sit under a tree, or just sit in your backyard with your eyes closed and listen. Earthing.

If you don't have time for that, just wiggle your toes or stomp your feet and pay close attention to the feeling of the vibration left behind from your movement. I do this anytime I feel anxious or panicky. Just bring your attention to your feet in anyway that you can. It helps get you out of your head and into your body. Breathe fully and feel the breath move through your body all the way to your feet. It also helps to sit on your hands. Brings you to the present moment.

Turn on any music, close your eyes, and listen to one instrument at a time. It's amazing how calming this is. When you have been listening carefully for only one instrument for a while, switch to another.

Guided meditations are another great way to center. I have recorded some of my own, and they are available on my website. Also, just repeating mantras helps. Close your eyes and repeat "*I am.*" "*I am grounded.*" "*I am safe.*" etc.

Keep a stone in your pocket or on a piece of jewelry. Hematite, smoky quartz, and black tourmaline are wonderful grounding stones. Just pick one up and see how it feels to you.

If you are someone who wants to learn how to be a medium, it's even more important to meditate. I started out having deceased family members, and even friend's family members come to me in my dreams. Meditation is a way to empty out your own monkey brain thoughts, which frees you up to be more receptive to others. It even makes you more receptive to your own intuition. It's really important to be present. Keep a dream journal, because the more you start delving into this intuitive psychic work, the more your dreams will have meaning. Journal work for any intuitive "hit" you get. Synchronicities and signs. You'll start to notice them more and more. And make sure you tell the Universe thank you when you do.

Cutting Cords

The practice of "Ho'oponopono" has become a very popular new age healing technique. It is an ancient Hawaiian practice for forgiveness. The word translates into English as "Correction."

When you are feeling "stuck" in life, use the mantra: "I'm sorry. Please forgive me. I love you. Thank you."

Repeat these phrases and more of your "stuff" starts coming up. With more clarity, you can then start to work through it. You begin to understand where your energetic blocks are. Ask yourself: *Why should I be sorry? What do I have to be sorry for? What do I need forgiveness for right now? What do I have to be grateful for? When I say, "I love you," am I really feeling it? Why? What is in the way?*

It also brings about stillness and calm and quiets the chaos in the mind. Try it. It's amazing what starts coming up for you that you didn't even know was there. And *then* you can cut cords to clear it.

Imagine you have cords— like garden hoses of energy— connecting your energy to others' energy, back and forth between anyone we are attached to in some way. They can be healthy or unhealthy, and some are very draining. I always imagine these cords to be attached at our hearts. There are major cords between spouses, lovers, siblings, parents, and close friends.

And there are minor cords between our co-workers, clients, teachers, bosses, etc.

You can begin a meditation by grounding yourself into the earth, and then imagine someone you want to cut cords with sitting across from you. You can see the energy pulsating back and forth on the cord that connects you to this person. Imagine that you use scissors, your breath, or a giant saw to cut them. You can even ask for help from a guide or a loved one in spirit to help you do it. You can either choose to cut all negative cords and get rid of them completely, or cut the negative cords and re-form positive ones. Some are attached to chakras, called aka cords. You can cut them away from each chakra with breath or sound.

The Sailboat

"I descended the cold stone stairs in the dark. It was creepy here, I'm not going to lie. It smelled musty, and everything was wet with water dripping from some unknown, unseen place. Each time I brushed up against the stone wall next to me, it was cold and made my sleeve feel damp. I made my way down to the bottom of the stairs and came to a hallway lined with doors. I didn't know which one to open. I felt uncomfortable here and I was worried about what would be on the other side of each door. I walked further down the hall and stopped in front of door #17. The number seventeen had no significant meaning to me. I'm not sure why I felt compelled to stop here, or why I felt that this was the door to open. I opened the door feeling very sure of my decision and not afraid. In the shadows of the dungeon-like room, a soft spotlight from above revealed a small plastic toy sailboat sitting in the middle of the room on the floor. It was blue and white, and very clean and shiny, completely in contrast to the dark space where it was sitting. Just then, the fuzzy image of a little girl began to materialize. She picked up the boat and was playing with it. The boat was so clear and she was so fuzzy. It was hard to see what she looked like. Just as quickly as I arrived there, it was time to go. I came back up the same stairs I went down, leaving with more questions than I had when I arrived."

-JUNE 16, 2016

Energetic Protection

What is an empath? An empath is someone who feels others' energy and emotions, sometimes very deeply. This becomes a huge problem when you're just walking around the grocery store and a stranger that you cross paths with in the produce section is having a bad day. You leave the store irritated and feeling like *you're* having a bad day. You aren't sure why you're feeling this way, and you honestly didn't even notice until you stopped to think about it. *"I was having a great day. Why do I feel like this?"* You picked it up from someone else. The new-age term for lower-vibration people is "energy vampire," and I kind of really love this term. Here you are, buying groceries as your radiant self, and some energy sucker sees, notices, and is subconsciously attracted to your light at a soul level.

I personally really have never felt like I was an empath. Not that I don't feel others' energy, but I think it has been very rare for me to pick up another person's and carry it with me. I feel like I have always known what's mine, and even though I can show empathy, I don't absorb the energy as much as some. But as far as my clients go, I understand that this is a real problem. Some people feel the whole world. Every negative bit of energy out there, they absorb it all and they feel it so deeply. You must learn how to protect yourself from the energy of others, the energy of spirits, and also the energy of your space: your home, your car, your office, and so on.

Everything is energy. I am energy. You are energy. Your thoughts are energy. Spirits are energy. The space around us is energy. Plants and trees are energy. The food we eat is energy. Even books, furniture, and objects are energy.

External energies and thoughts have the ability to cloud, drain, and toxify your energetic space. It is essential that your energy field stays clear, pure and as "you" as possible in order to hold your own space, and secure it from intrusion from negative energy that you might encounter throughout the day.

The best thing you can do is to stay positive. Like attracts like. Energy goes where attention flows. Surround yourself with like-minded people, stay away from needy energy vampires who just "take." Ask yourself, *"Is this mine?"* If it isn't, clear it and get rid of it.

Read the following exercise and then close your eyes, hands palm up:

I want you to imagine the vines and roots again coming from your feet and encircling the earth's crust. You are grounded into the earth. You are safe. These roots begin glowing until you are glowing in white light. It moves from your feet to your shoulders, all the way up to the crown of your head. It's like a bubble or a mist that surrounds you. You notice that it connects from above, through the trees, to the top of your head, and all the way to your roots and through the earth. How does it feel in this bubble?

The best way to protect yourself from negative energy of others is to meditate, with either a guided meditation or just by sitting quietly and taking deep breaths. Use grounding exercises, breathing exercises, and yoga. It also helps to cross your arms, legs, or even your fingers to give yourself a visual of protecting your own energy. You can imagine a bubble or circle of protection around you. The "I'm rubber and you're glue..." from middle school actually has great meaning and intention. The bubble you create around yourself might also be made of shiny mirror material that bounces back to the person with negative energy. Try visualizing protective colors around you, usually a white or blue light that surrounds you. Maybe you could even try a healing coating of paint or a barrier or wall that you build up between you and the rest of the world. It also helps to balance your chakras. You can ask for help from guides, angels, God, Jesus, Buddha, ancestors, Spirit (whoever you connect with). Take a shower or bathe in salt water (Epsom salt bath). Water is amazing for clearing energy. Even just washing your hands or face helps. Shake the water off your hands and visualize the energy splashing away. Drink plenty of water. Amethyst, black tourmaline, smoky quartz, and labradorite are great stones for protection. Essential oils such as Frankincense, Myrrh, Juniper, Pine, and Sandalwood work, too. Carry a crystal, gemstone, amulet, pentacle, cross, rosary, talisman, or good luck charm with you.

Red Blood

"There was a huge tree with a hollowed trunk with a space big enough to squeeze into. Inside, the walls were made out of stone and not wood. I was in a cave and not a tree. It felt cozy in here and when I peered out of my cave, I could see out into the night of an open field, and I could see millions of stars in the sky. As the stars dissolved and the sun came out, I emerged from my cave and into the bright field. Through the clearing, I could see a path in the woods— so I walked toward it to follow my path.

I walked down a dirt trail in the forest with a river to my right. It was a sunny afternoon. I could hear birds chirping and there was a slight breeze blowing through the trees. The branches blocked the sunlight with their leaves as they moved and cast shadows. The river was flowing up, toward something, not down and away.

"Try stepping into the river." Eryn said.

I turned to my right, stepped down a rocky embankment, and put my bare feet into the cold flowing water. I proceeded in, walking in up to my knees, my hips, my chest, my shoulders. The water was not cold, nor warm but felt exactly the same temperature as my body. Like air. I lay back and the water covered my hair and my ears. I floated in this space, like a deprivation tank, but looking up at the trees and the sun as I floated gently by.

Eryn asked, "Do you see anything coming up ahead of you?"

"No, I'm just enjoying the flow." I replied.

"I feel like you need a boat. Try imagining a boat." She said.

A canoe appeared and started floating next to me. I raised my head from the water and climbed aboard. I wasn't wet. I sat up looking at my surroundings— nothing had changed and there was nothing ahead but more river and more trees. Suddenly my boat turned slightly to the left and slid to a stop over the greenest Technicolor grass I've ever seen. Thick blades that looked more like plastic than grass.

"My boat stopped" I said.

Eryn replied, "Great. Go ahead and step out."

I stepped over the side of the boat and onto the grass. I looked down at my feet. They didn't look like my feet. They looked bigger, wider.

"Did you get out of the boat on the left side or the right side?" She asked.

"The left side." I said

"Okay great, I'm with you. Is there something different about the grass you're standing on?" She asked.

"Yes! It looks abnormally green and it looks like it's almost made out of plastic!"

"Yes it does!" She exclaimed. "Do you see anyone?"

I looked around but it seemed I was alone in an open clearing in the woods. I was just standing in a big field next to my canoe. Suddenly I saw someone walking toward me. He came through a mist— well... not a mist actually—more like heat waves, like what it looks like when you look through the top of a fire. (I've seen this in Salem before at Forest River Park, but I wasn't sure what that meant.) This person was a massive, tall man. He was huge and stocky. He had orange-red hair, tattered clothing, and was barefoot. He wore a smile on his face as he approached me.

"I see a huge tall man." I said.

"What is this man's name?" Eryn asked.

"I don't know. I just get a feeling that he is my ancestor, like a great

uncle."

Suddenly, I saw that he brought friends with him, who followed behind him and came through the distorted air. These people were all abnormally tall. The women had very long hair. Everything about them was tall and long. They all smiled at me.

"There's more people with him. They are all very tall." I said.

"Oh! I know where you are! This will be fun, I've never been here before. Follow them!" She said.

The man gave me a smirk and turned around as if to tell me to go with them. We walked down the path in the woods, the river still flowing to our right. We walked and walked in silence.

"Have you reached somewhere yet?" She asked.

"No, still walking."

We continued on through the woods and came to a clearing. There were many people there, including kids, bustling around and working, carrying items, being busy. A city. Although this city hadn't been built yet. There were piles of huge wooden beams, smaller pieces of wood, and other building materials laying in piles where homes should be. When we walked up to the edge of these piles, everyone stopped working and smiled at us before continuing on with their work.

"There are piles of wood." I told her.

"What is the wood for?"

"To build homes, cabins. To build a city. But not today. We are just passing through."

So we walked through this place bustling with people and smiled as we continued on. Up ahead on the hillside, I saw a huge castle. "Well, that's cliché," I thought.

"There's a castle." I said.

"Oh great! I was hoping you'd get there soon!" She exclaimed.

I walked closer to it and observed that it looked like a trite fairytale castle, made of huge gray stones. I walked by the outside wall looking around, and felt the unusually cold rock with my hands as I passed. There were red flags high above the multiple towers. And the cobblestone pathway leading to the castle's door was lined with red banners.

"Go inside." She told me.

I didn't use the massive front door. Leaving my tall uncle behind, I walked up a stone staircase off to the right and through an archway that had no door, like I lived here. As I walked through the archway and into the castle, I looked down at myself and saw that I was suddenly wearing a beautiful red velvet gown and robe. I looked at my hands and they didn't look like mine. I was wearing a huge red ruby ring.

"Everything here is red." I said.

My gown, the furniture, the rugs that covered the stone floors were all shades of red, with a bit of gold mixed in.

"Keep looking around and walk wherever you feel you should go."

So of course being in the cliché castle, I headed straight for the winding spiral staircase of the tallest tower. I walked up and up, my red gown dragging behind me up each step. When I reached the top, there was a huge wooden door layered with wrought iron, complete with a round pull handle.

"I'm in the tower." I said.

"Great. Go inside."

I opened the heavy door and saw a deathly pale girl with even paler blonde hair wearing a white gown, sitting against the far wall, holding her knees to her chest.

"There's a girl in here. Very pale. Almost like an albino." I said.

"What does she need?"

"I'm not sure."

I looked around the room. Did I put her here? I suddenly felt a sharp burning pain in my right arm and looked down at it.

"There's stitches in my right arm."

"What part of your arm? What do they look like?" She asked.

"They are long vertical lines that begin at my wrist and extend up my forearm. They are on the underside of my arm, and also at the top. It's as if something sharp had gone straight through it to the other side. The stitches themselves look more like shoelaces than medical stitches. And they each end with a neat bow tied at my wrist on both sides. And I can feel it."

"Did someone hurt you? Did you hurt yourself? What weapon was the wound made with?"

"I'm really not sure." I said.

I know that my physical body was lying safe on a table, but my arm burned, an icy cold burn. I could physically feel this wound on my arm. "I should untie these stitches." I thought. I was still standing in the center of this tower room. The little girl sat at the far side of the round space on the stone floor with her arms wrapped around her knees, and now her forehead rested on top of them.

Carefully with the fingers of my left hand, I pulled the loop free at the top of the stitches. Deep burgundy-red blood spilled from my arm, down my bright red velvet gown, and onto the gray stone floor. The blood flowed like a river and travelled across the room and under the pale girl on the floor. As the blood flowed to her, she became vibrant and glowing. Her pale white blond hair turned a golden yellow blonde, and she had color in her face and cheeks. I spoke out loud what I was seeing.

"Does losing the blood affect you? What is the girl doing now?" Eryn asked.

"No, I seem completely fine. Like I have plenty of blood to spare. The girl is dancing and twirling around the room in her pretty white dress. She smiled at me and hopped happily down the stairs and left

the castle."

"Who was she?"

"I think she was a part of me." I said.

"I think she was too. And you set her free."

Hmm. And there was so much red, I thought. The color of the root chakra, the color of safety. Permission to be. Freedom and light. Stepping into my gifts and freeing the little girl who used to believe, who had her vibrancy and color drained out of her. Healing her with my wounds."

-AUGUST 8, 2017

The "Clairs"

T he word paranormal just means "not normal." Experiences that can't be explained. Everyone has instances where something happened that they can't explain, like feeling goosebumps for no reason, hair standing up on the back of your neck, or movement or shadows out of the corner of your eye. Maybe you hear someone call your name and no one is there, or you smell a flower, cigarette, perfume, etc. with no known source. Have you ever experienced a weird taste in your mouth when you haven't eaten anything? Or have a feeling that you shouldn't drive your regular route home from work and find out there was an accident that way?

Everybody is psychic. An example I used before is that some people are born musical prodigies and some people have to take lessons, and really practice. Some have a little natural born talent, and then build upon that. I just chose to work on this part of myself.

I've also mentioned in a previous chapter that I don't like the word "psychic" because Hollywood has ruined it. I prefer to use the word "intuitive". All mediums are intuitive, not all intuitives are mediums. Channels are another name for medium. You are the middle-man, just giving someone a message from someone else. And if you're really great at it, you're just delivering mail without opening the package first.

We all have different "Clairs." Most everyone has heard of clairvoyance, but it's less common to know of our other "clair" senses.

Clairvoyance means "Clear seeing". It's like when you daydream. Like a picture or a movie in your mind's eye. This could be a person, object, color, shape, or even a written word.

Choose an object in the room, and then close your eyes and see it in your mind. Look at the details, the colors, the textures, and bring it in closer. Now imagine you are in your own living room. What details do you see?

Clairaudience means "Clear hearing." This is hearing words, music, and other sounds in your mind. Everyone knows what it's like to get a song stuck in your head out of nowhere, sometimes those songs have meaning.

Close your eyes, swallow, and listen to the sound it makes. Was it louder than you thought? Doing exercises like this while you go about your day, listening to the sounds the world makes, will strengthen this inner sense.

Clairsentience means "Clear feeling." It is very much the same as being an empath, feeling another's emotions, and thoughts. It can also be feeling someone else's physical pain. Feeling like you're going to cry during a reading, getting a sharp pain in your knee when your knee is fine, etc.

Claircognizance means "Clear knowing." When you "just know" something and you have no idea why. It didn't come from you. That "gut feeling". Something feels right or wrong. Car problems, taking a different route, knowing a family member is sick. Have trust and faith to listen to that inner-knowing daily.

Clairalience means "Clear smelling," smelling something that is obviously not in your physical space.

Close your eyes and imagine you are cooking dinner and you smell garlic and onions. Now imagine you are sitting at the ocean and you can smell the salty air. Now imagine you can smell a campfire, or fresh laundry out of the dryer.

Clairaugustine means "Clear tasting." It is similar to clairalience, but relates to taste instead of smell. I tend to think that chefs do this. They can taste each ingredient as they add it to their recipe.

Close your eyes and imagine you can taste chocolate, now imagine the taste of lemonade, now some savory Mexican food.

The following is a helpful exercise/meditation to help discover your most intuitive senses:

You're in a garden. You have your hands in the dirt. You decide to pick a flower.

What does it look like? What type of flower is it? What color is it? What does it smell like? What does it feel like? Pick a petal. Is it soft? Is it edible? Can you taste the petals? What does it taste like? Sweet? Bitter?

You leave the garden and walk down the sidewalk. You can hear a lawn mower.

Where is the sound coming from? The right? The left? Maybe behind you?

You can feel the wind on your face as you walk. A child dropped a basketball and you can hear it bouncing toward you. Reach down and pick it up.

Can you feel the texture of the ball? Can you see the color? Is it sun faded or new?

You hand the ball back to this child.

Do you know their name?

Spend some time being present here. You can choose to sit

down, or walk some more. See what other senses you experience.

In order to start getting a feel for which "clairs" are your strongest, the most important thing is to stay in the present moment. This is why daily meditations are so helpful with psychic development. You miss important signs and "hits" when you're busy being human and living in the past or the future. Also, try making your practice a game. Guess who is calling you before you look at the phone. Guess which color of car is going to drive by next. Guess how someone is feeling before you see them by practicing feeling each other's energy.

Journaling is also very important. Write down each time you're right, and express gratitude and tell the Universe thank you. Don't worry about it if you're wrong. It doesn't mean anything, so don't give up. You're *practicing*.

Try automatic writing. Sit down with your journal, do a quick grounding meditation and then write down a question that you have. Then answer them. You can either put your pen to paper and close your eyes and let the pen flow, or you can intuitively receive the answer in your mind's eye and write it down. You'll also be surprised to find answers and messages— words that stand out to you—as you flip through books (try using this one!) and even social media, just as you would during a tarot reading.

There are many types of fun exercises you can do: Write down different shapes, colors, numbers, or letters on index cards and shuffle them either by type or all together. Try to intuitively guess which card you have and flip it over to see if you're right. You'll be amazed at how much better you start to become when you do this constantly.

Have friends send you photos of friends or family that you don't know. See what you can intuitively sense about this person from this photograph about them. You can even try doing a meditation where you meet this person in a coffee shop and ask them questions.

You can do the same thing using any object that someone owns, and see what you sense about this person from their possession. This is called psychometry. Keys work really well for this exercise.

A Poem

Refreshing water

Cold and Cleansing

Weightlessness

Moving only forward

Merging into myself

Carefree

Staying above water

A reflection I don't see

Slow heavy circles

Remembering me

-JUNE 25, 2016

Astrology And Moon Cycles

I 've always really been into astrology. As a teenager, I went to a place in Eastern Washington called Table Mountain, and I met all of these amazing astronomers, both amateurs and professionals. I spent the whole night looking through their telescopes, asking questions, and purchasing my own star maps that night. I have always been really, really interested in the way the planets move and the way they affect us.

My 13 year old son and I attended an 8 week Astrology certification course with my friend and freaking amazing Astrologer, Veronica.

I also attended many workshops on moon cycles and ceremonies. Our bodies are mostly made up of water, so as the moon goes through its phases, those cycles affect us and everything else on this earth because the earth is also made up of mostly water. As I became more in tune with becoming a witch and hosting my own moon circles while in Seattle, I felt the strong importance of it.

You create change in your life through these ceremonies. They don't need to be a big deal, inviting friends over for a "proper" circle. You can create personal moon ceremonies and rituals in your own home by yourself. You want to hold intention with each moon cycle to create change, and you want to celebrate yourself, your goals, and your achievements.

Moon rituals are called Esbats. The word means "to frolic," and is the celebration of the moon. These ceremonies used to take place in Pagan times. They would celebrate nude to expose their body to the full moon and bathe in the moonlight. The moonlight was meant to be fuel to accomplish goals. Drawing down the moon to absorb the light energy, blessing yourself and others, and also to bless meaningful items. It's also a really good way to cleanse yourself, your belongings, and any secret items that you have, such as your tarot cards, jewelry, and crystals.

Your intention always aligns with the sun, so the dark moon phase is this stillpoint, like placid water, and it aligns with the internal so that we can reset, let go, and surrender. Set new intentions and ground when the sun and the moon align, it's time to heal and let go. The new moon is for resetting your intention each month, and the full moon is for expansiveness. Take inventory. What was accomplished? Your new moon is for intention setting, for growing, for planting, for setting momentum, and the full moon is to celebrate, to check and reset your destination to be sure you're headed the right direction. I believe that the new moon is internal and the full moon is both internal and external.

The solar cycle is 365 days, a full year. The lunar cycle is 28 days. There are 13 lunar cycles in one solar cycle. The moon switches astrological signs every 2 1/3 days, just like a clock.

Sabbats are solar gatherings. The Sabbats are for celebrating the sun: The Winter Solstice (Yule), the Spring Equinox (Ostara), the Summer Solstice (Litha), and the Autumn Equinox (Mabon).

There are also quarter days, or midpoints, in between:

Imbolc, marking the first stirrings of spring, aligns with the modern observance of Groundhog Day;

Beltane, marking the first stirrings of summer, aligns with May

Day;

Lughnasdh, marking the first stirrings of Autumn, celebrates harvest;

And Samhain, marking the first stirrings of winter, aligns with Halloween and the Day of the Dead.

Ritual guides us to sink into rhythm, celebration, acknowledgment, and support.

I feel it is very important to bring in a relationship with the moon under the forces of nature. It is equally important to know what the planets are doing in correlation to your own signs. You have an entire astrological chart to use as a personal map as you navigate through life. Your birth chart is essentially a snap-shot of the sky above you at the exact moment and place you were born.

When someone asks, "What's your sign?" the sign you likely know is your sun sign, but you are so much more than just that. It is equally important to at least know your moon sign, and also your rising sign (the sign that was coming up next on the horizon as you came into this world). Each planet in the sky plays a role in who you are. You can really go down the astrological rabbit hole and learn which houses your planets lay, as each house has specific meaning in your life.

When you match up what is happening currently with the planets and overlap them with the planets on your own chart, it gives you guidance day-by-day, week-by-week, and even year-by-year. So if you're having a really terrible day and you look at your chart, you'll see exactly why. If somebody said something to you that bothers you so much more than it would on any other day, you can look at your chart and see what the stars and planets are doing and you can find out why you felt that way.

I am a Pisces, but it means much more to know that I have Cancer rising, and my moon is in Gemini. I also have a lot of planets in Virgo which gives me organizational skills that a typical Pisces usually lacks. As I have been on this intuitive path in my work, I use astrology so much more than I used to. Your astrological chart can tell you exactly why you are here, what your purpose is, and help you move forward and have direction every day.

Use Your Gifts

"I walked down to the same gazebo where I met the middle eastern man who reminded me of Aladdin. I haven't "heard from" that man since that day. Instead my "uncle" was there to greet me this time. I felt him tell me his name is Thomas, perhaps Tom for short. He said, "Use your gifts," and told me to wear my shattuckite crystal and carry a mystic merlinite stone. I thanked him and he smiled."

-OCTOBER 10, 2017

Metaphysical Tools

Pendulums are one of my favorite tools to help guide your intuition. Each time you pick up the pendulum, you need to find out what yes and what no is for you. It could be completely different every time you pick up the same pendulum. If it's a different pendulum, you definitely need to ask what is yes, and what is no.

Once you know what your yes and no are, you can use it to ask spirits questions, or you can use it to ask daily questions about your life.

You can ask if it's going to rain tomorrow, and it will tell you.

You can use it to find your keys, by drawing a diagram of your home. Hold your pendulum over the piece of paper and ask where your keys are, and it will swing to that room. And then if you want to get even more detailed with it, you can draw just that room and see if you can find out where it is in that room.

You can make pie charts, too. For instance, when I was going to move back to Seattle, I didn't know if it was the right move for me, so I made a chart that said Salem, Seattle, and Hawaii (just for good measure). When I asked the pendulum, "Where should I move?" it swung toward Seattle.

There's an old wives tale that if you put a ring on a necklace and hold it above a pregnant woman's belly, you can ask if they're having a boy or a girl. You would say, "Show me boy," and then

"Show me girl," and then "What am I having?" When I was pregnant and living in Salem, I had about ten women all come into a room and silently write down on a piece of paper what their answer showed. Every single slip of paper said girl, and I had a girl.

You can also use your pendulum to ask spirits questions, as I taught before. You can ask if there's someone in the room with you, or any kind of yes or no questions you can think of. This works by picking up on your own energy. It's helping you use your own intuition. When you ask a pendulum if someone you're dating is the right match for you, you already know the answer to that question deep down inside. If you're asking the pendulum where you lost your car keys, subconsciously you know where you left your car keys. If you're asking the pendulum whether you're going to have a good day tomorrow, your soul already knows the answer to that question. Again, pendulums are my favorite intuitive tool.

Dowsing rods can work using the same intuitive energy. Try walking with them gently in your hands and when they cross, it shows that there is a disruption in energy. Maybe there's a water source below you, or the fluorescent light above you is putting off EMF— or maybe there's a spirit standing in front of you. Maybe you don't know which is the case, but it's definitely interesting.

You also can use them just as you would a pendulum, asking for yes and no. Perhaps they cross for yes, and spread apart for no. Or you can use them to ask a spirit if they would like to speak to a specific person in the room, and they'll slowly point in someone's direction. (Yeah, sometimes that can be a bit creepy.)

I've already talked about EMF detectors, temperature guns, flashlights, audio recorders, and spirit boxes in previous chapters, but these are also great divination tools with a scientific edge, if that helps your left brain.

Crystal balls are not the Hollywood "let me gaze into my ball and see the future" thing. A crystal ball is meant to give your eyes something to focus on as you use your intuition. As you look into your mind's eye, sometimes it's easier to give yourself some soft focus and something to see, rather than closing your eyes. It's the same thing as seeing shapes in the clouds in the sky. It's also the same as reading tea leaves. You're seeing something in that crystal ball that isn't really there, but in your mind's eye, you can make out the shapes in that ball.

Another popular method is using a watch— like for hypnosis— the pocket watch that swings back and forth. All that watch is doing is giving your eyes something to focus on so that you can go within and be present, and pay attention to what is inside instead of what is outside.

Ouija boards have been used for centuries. They were originally used for very specific purposes, for a very controlled séance ritual. So many people are scared to death of ouija boards. They have a very bad reputation, and everybody thinks they're evil. I have heard superstitions saying that you need to burn them or bury them in your backyard.

I do not believe that any of these things are true. The reason that ouija boards have such a bad gut reaction for people when they see them is because of their first encounter with one. When Parker Brothers decided to make the ouija board a board game, it created havoc amongst teenagers. Teens would purchase a ouija board and use it for the sole purpose of scaring their friends.

If you are using a board or any metaphysical divination tool for a negative purpose, you're going to get a negative result. If you are going to use this board for the best intentions, to contact a loved one or to get more information from a spirit that has already been contacting you, then they are really great tools. Projecting negative intentions to scare somebody, is like inviting a spirit to scare somebody. I really believe in lower vibrational energies. They're around, and they're looking for lower vibration energy people to cling to. When they see that opportunity, and your intention, and you're using this board, that's what they're going to do. If you're using this tool out of love then you will get love in return. So there is nothing wrong with the ouija board. It is a tool just like any other tool that you are using to communicate with the dead, as long as you're doing it in the right way with the most positive intention.

Crystals are another important metaphysical tool. There are crystals,minerals and other stones that have unique purposes, and I believe if you use them the right way, they will really help you. There are stones for different elements: fire, water, air, earth. It's best to cleanse those stones with their elements. You bury earth stones in the earth, you put water stones in the water. You can use sage for the fire stones, and the full moon for air stones.

Clear quartz is a really good clean slate for any kind of intention. You can tell your clear quartz what you would like help with that day, and then put it in your pocket.

Obsidian really helps suck negative energy away, so it's a really good protection stone.

Amethyst is kind of the free-for-all good for anything stone, kind of like lavender in the essential oil world. It's good for protection, dreaming, meditation, and for connecting with your guides.

I use a stone called shattukite a lot, and also one called mystic merlin. Both help with spirit communication. And I think I've previously said that I like to carry some black tourmaline with me. It's really good for grounding.

There is a green stone called moldavite that is made from the heat and the pressure from a meteor hitting the earth. It's a strange crystal. You'll have to feel it for yourself.

This is just a small list of my favorite crystals. There are many resources out there to help you decide which type of crystal would be right for you, Be sure to visit a crystal shop and feel the energy of each to begin or add to your collection.

Tarot And Oracle Cards

I don't read tarot cards "by the book" they way many readers do. I don't use specific spreads, such as the popular Celtic Cross for reading someone's past, present, and future. If all you do is read the book, you are reading somebody else's interpretation of that card. You are reading what the artist wanted that card to mean. When I see a card, it's like going to an art museum. People see fine art and they ask, "What is this artist trying to say to me today?" Everybody who sees that same painting is going to see something different. So when I read a card, it is going to mean something completely different from one person to the next. I am reading my client's energy, not the card itself. The card is a tool to help me move in the right direction.

Tarot will increase your natural intuitive ability. It works through your "clairs" and helps trigger right brain action. Think of a Rorschach InkBlot Test or looking at a painting. *"What do you see?"* Tarot is a treasure-trove of myth, archetype, and ancient symbolism to connect you with your higher self.

The deck: Most decks consist of 78 cards: 22 Major Arcana and 56 Minor Arcana.

The Minor Arcana consists of four "suits," just like a deck of playing cards. Long ago, playing cards were used for fortune tell-

164

ing.. Each suit of the tarot correlates with a different playing card: Pentacles=Diamonds, Cups=Hearts, Swords=Spades, and Wands=Clubs.

Tarot reflects the energies and cycles of human consciousness. It dates back to the 16th century, with symbols and archetypes dating back to ancient Greece, Rome, and Egypt, as well as early Jewish and Celtic origins.

The four Minor Arcana Suits are:

Pentacles- (Earth) Represents grounding, strength, money, success issues.

Wands- (Fire) Represents passion, spiritual issues, creative endeavors, goals.

Cups- (Water) Represents love, emotional issues, passion, relationships.

Swords-(Air) Represents conflict, thought patterns, clarity, things to work on.

The following is a list of Major Arcana Cards and a short summary of what each card personally means to me:

0.   The Fool: Being blissfully naive

1.   Magician: Using your gifts

2.   High Priestess: Following signs from spirit

3.   The Empress: Creating a new cycle

4.   The Emperor: Ending an old cycle

5.   Hierophant: Spiritual learning

6.   Lovers: Partnership

7.   Chariot: Determination and leadership

8.   Justice: Creating balance

9.   Hermit: Reflection and rest

10.   Wheel of Fortune: Taking a chance

11.   Strength: Drawing power from past experiences

12.   Hanged Man: Stagnation

13.   Death: Change

14.   Temperance: Creating flow

15.   Devil: Having a little too much fun

16.   Tower: Huge earth-shattering event

17.   Star: Connecting the dots

18.   Moon: Shining light on a shadow

19.   Sun: An astrological cycle

20.   Judgment: Speaking your truth

21.   World: Mastery

An oracle deck doesn't have a specific structure of suits. These cards contain different messages, mantras, ways of life, and advice, and they usually have a lot of really gorgeous artwork. When reading oracle cards, simply read the companion guide and read your message. There's not much intuition involved, at least the way I use them. I think they are perfect for personal daily messages. When you pull an oracle card, it's easier to read the message that someone else had intended than it is to attempt to read your own tarot cards. It's not impossible, but it's more difficult to read your own energy. Oracle cards are great for when you are needing a little bit of advice, a little bit of daily guidance, and it's for you personally and not necessarily a client — although I do occasionally pull oracle cards for clients if it feels right. Oracle cards come in all sorts of unique themes by different artists. I personally have a witch oracle deck, a spirit guides deck, and many more. There's even kitten oracle cards, and funny uplifting ones. Whatever you love, there's probably an oracle deck for it.

It is really important to cleanse your all of your cards between readings. You can use sage or sea salt. It's always best to begin with some kind of meditation or grounding exercise.

When you first start to use tarot, simply begin by looking at a card and let something catch your eye. Ask what this image reminds you of.

How does it feel? Does it feel vibrant? Calm? Nervous? Creepy? Ecstatic? Warm? Cool? Freezing? Intellectual? Sexual? Loving? Angry?

Try making up a story about the image that you see. Maybe there is a family on the card— *What is this family doing, and what could this possibly mean for the person that you're reading, and the energy that you were already picking up about them?*

Go with your very first thought. When you hesitate, you're letting your left brain and your ego take over. There is no such thing as right or wrong. If you aren't getting anything at all, try closing your eyes, breathe, center yourself, and then try again. Practice reading as much as possible. Read for friends, read for family members, pull a card every day for yourself and practice that way. The more you do it, the more it just becomes second nature and after a while you'll find that you can give amazing readings and you don't even need cards anymore!

The Wildflowers

"I went back to the huge tree of life with the opening in the trunk. Inside was different this time. It was not a cave, but a room with a small desk and a lamp. The walls were wooden, the inside of the tree. From this small warm room there were wooden stairs that led up, and there was another set of stairs that led down. I decided to take the stairs down. I came to an opening in the tree and could see bright sunlight and another beautiful green field. I emerged from the tree into the sunlight and spent some time feeling the energy of nature. The field was filled with wildflowers of every color, and bees were buzzing around pollinating them. I danced and twirled barefoot in the grass in a long pale blue dress. My hair was long golden brown curls that bounced as I skipped around.

"Do you see a trail anywhere?" Brooke asked.

I looked around, and yes, I saw a wide dirt trail in the distance that looked like it was worn with horse tracks. I knew it led to a village. I really didn't feel like going that direction, I'd rather stay in the field, but I was instructed to go, so I gloomily started walking. I came to a small village that seemed like it had no color. Everything was gray, even the crooked cobblestone roads. I'm not sure what year it was, but it seemed like centuries ago. There were people milling about doing chores and running errands. Women were throwing buckets of dirty water out their second story windows, and hanging laundry to dry high above the streets. Men chatted out on the street near their horses and carriages. As I walked down the street, I could feel the warmth coming from these small narrow homes, and I could smell food cooking in cauldrons on an open fire.

I walked into my home where I lived with my mother. She needed me to help with the household chores: cooking, laundry, sweeping. I wanted to be back in the grassy field, in nature with the flowers. I didn't like the dark colorless village. She sent me to the butcher shop across the street, and I said hello to the butcher's son, who was my age, helping his father behind the counter. I then had flashes of memories with this man throughout the years. He loved me and I loved him. He wanted to marry me, have children with me, and even though he was a gentle soul and I didn't want to hurt him, marriage just wasn't for me. I knew I needed to be my own person. I could feel his sadness when I looked at his hurt face.

I spent my time in the wildflower fields. I would pick these flowers and arrange them into beautiful bouquets to sell in a small wooden flower stand that the butcher's son built for me on the street corner of the village. I also instinctively knew how to use these flowers to make medicines, tinctures, oils, essences, and salves. This was how I made a living and I was happy. It would seem a lonely life, but I wasn't lonely. My neighbors were great friends and loved how much my flowers and herbs helped people. It livened up the village with color and light, outside and in.

I watched the rest of this story as an outsider, looking from above. I watched this woman become old and gray on that street corner. I watched her collapse as neighbors surrounded her and lay her gently on the ground and held her as she died.

And then I was back in the little cozy room in the tree. The man that I met in a previous journey who called himself my great uncle was sitting at the small desk with the lamp. He looked massive sitting in such a tiny space. He motioned that we should take the staircase going up. So I climbed to the top of the small wooden staircase and out of the opening in the tree trunk to a huge building—a palace maybe— with marble floors and white pillars that were so tall I couldn't see the top of them as they disappeared into the clouds above. It looked like a Greek or Roman temple of some sort. Across this massive space was a fountain flowing with crystal clear sparkling water. It was as if the water itself was glowing. I understood that this water was energy. Life force energy as water, just as it was when I channel it for my clients. This reiki energy that was the purest, cleanest energy there ever was. This man, my guide, smiled and motioned for me to take a drink. It didn't seem right to dip my hands in the water, but I looked down at my hands and they were clean and glowing too. I scooped up the water in my palms and took a refreshing sip. I expected magick and fireworks, but nothing happened. I felt good, but as if nothing had changed. We walked back to the tree, back to the small room, and said goodbye as I climbed out and came back into the room I had left."

-OCTOBER 16, 2017

Receiving And Deciphering Spirit Messages

I t is important to do some kind of ritual before opening up to spirit communication. It could be a simple few deep breaths, or a grounding meditation. Project the intention of protecting your own energy and expanding your aura.

Here is my meditation for connecting with your loved ones in spirit:

"Find a comfortable position, either lying down or sitting up with your palms face up. Take a few deep breaths in and out as you relax.

Imagine that you are expanding the light of your own energy, your aura. As you take a moment to center yourself and focus on your breath, you become a beacon of light shining brightly so that those in spirit are able to recognize that you are open to communication. Next, take a few moments here to ground your energy into the Earth, perhaps imagining that you have vines wrapping around your ankles and anchoring you to the core below.. You feel safe and connected as you find a place of peace.

When you are ready, invite spirit to come to you. Someone you are hoping to hear from, someone you have been missing—a loved one, a family member, a friend who is now on the other side. Invite them to come close to you. Imagine them standing in front of you or sitting in a chair in front of you. Begin paying attention to the things that you are seeing, hearing, and feeling.

You don't need a medium or a psychic to connect to your loved ones in spirit; it is an ability we all have and is a connection that we can all make.

As you see the smiling face of your loved one in front of you, feel what it's like to be in their presence, in their space. Concentrate on your connection with them. What do they want to tell you? Ask them questions and share your thoughts. Breathe as you quietly trust the impressions that you are receiving. Your light is connected to their light as you communicate between worlds.

When you are ready to finish, express your gratitude and say goodbye. Take a few more deep breaths to center yourself before opening your eyes. It is then helpful to write down your feelings, and messages you received in your journal."

There are different types of spirit energy. An intelligent spirit can communicate with you, and he or she knows that you are there. You can ask questions and receive answers such as when I used to use ghost hunting equipment. This is also the energy you're working with as a medium. This spirit is using their energy to send you messages.

Residual spirit energy is just leftover past energy that repeats itself over and over. No one is actually there. Their energy has just been left behind, imprinted. You hear a lot about someone seeing a ghost walk by and watching them walk through a wall that used to be a door. That's residual energy. And here's where it gets weird... I believe we all leave residual energy in places we frequent. I heard a story from a friend about the residual energy in her house from her real estate agent. She said she was trying to sell her home and her agent would show her home on a regular basis. One day, she saw her agent walk up the stairs and he wasn't there. Her real estate agent hadn't died. He had just been there so many times to show her house that he left his imprinted energy there. This is why it is really important to sage your home. Think about that... you could be haunting your old home somewhere and not even know it!

The next type of spirit energy is a poltergeist. Now this isn't like the "CarolAnn, CarolAnn!" like the movie. Poltergeist energy is the negative energy of a living person. This happens a lot when someone is living at a very low vibration, such as drug addicts, or people with mental health problems or severe depression. It is a person's own energy wreaking havoc. This swirling spiral of negativity can sometimes cause books to fly off shelves and other horror-movie ghostly stereotypes.

The last type of spirit energy is inhuman or demonic. I personally do not believe in demons. I think that as humans, some have good energy, and some have bad energy. When you pass away, that does not change. So when an evil serial killer dies, his energy stays the same. This is the type of energy that scratches you or pushes you down the stairs. Again, more horror movie stereotypes. I believe there is evil out there, but not the monsters that have never stepped foot on earth and are here to take your soul.

Also, I want to point out that so many people are scared of ghosts and I don't see a good reason for that. I think there is just as much good energy and high vibration on the other side as there is here on Earth. You probably aren't afraid to walk down the street or go to the grocery store in your neighborhood. Most people are not afraid they are going to run into a serial killer.

(And if so, they are living in a place of fear and not love, and are probably attracting that type of energy themselves.) So why do some believe that every ghost they run into on the street is going to be negative or scary? People and spirits are generally good. Most who have passed on are confused, maybe, but not evil.

One last tidbit on the topic of "scary ghosts": In general, cemeteries are not haunted. I don't believe spirits hang out in cemeteries or graveyards just because their bodies lay there. But I *do* believe that loved ones come with you when you have the intention of visiting them there. Do you want to know where I think is the most haunted type of place? Antique shops! Seriously. There's all sorts of crazy energy swirling around in there by spirits who are attached to their prized possessions. I think maybe they're interested to know who will take that item home and love it as they did.

I remember learning about quantum physics and how it relates to different dimensions when I took the class from TAPS Academy. They were talking about how there are no EVP's or any kind of evidence that anybody further than the 1800s is communicating with us. I don't know how true that is, but it really makes me think about how our energy could just be replaying over and over, until eventually it just disappears. Then I start getting really philosophical about what happens after we die, and whether we're really still here and how long you can communicate after you go. And once you're forgotten do you just disappear forever?

So how do spirits communicate with us? First and foremost, communication takes place through our intuition and our "clairs," if we just become present and watch and listen. They use sound, by using voices, high-pitched ringing, or knocking and tapping. They use scents and smells and hope we notice it. They bring us thoughts— either out loud or in our heads— that are clearly not our own. We have visions, dreams, conscious thought, messages through meditation, and just knowingness through them.

They also use electronics. They of course will use ghost hunting equipment that is meant for communicating, or even your TV or radio. They'll turn them on/off, or adjust the volume, or channels begin changing. Or a song will come on the radio when it was playing in your head moments before. They'll use your telephone. Maybe just a single phone ring and no one is ever there. They can also communicate through your clock— either it stopping at a time that has meaning, or showing you repetitive numbers— Seeing 11:11, 4:44, etc. Those are known as angel numbers and you'll begin to see them everywhere if you pay attention. Spirits also attempt to communicate by making lights flicker and bulbs going out completely.

Spirits also communicate by feel— by touching, tapping you, pulling your hair, pushing you, or putting pressure on your chest. A huge one I've noticed a lot is feeling as if you've walked through cobwebs when there is no way a spider could have made a web to cover such a large area. They communicate by changes in temperature, like hot or cold spots. Or you'll feel a breeze, goosebumps, hair raising, increased heartbeat, or feeling jumpy and having anxiety.

Spirits can also use objects to get your attention. They'll move something, or an object will appear out of nowhere that you swear wasn't there before. This happens a lot with family mementoes or important items that belonged to your deceased family member. I've even heard instances of people finding letters from a loved one in a drawer that they didn't know was there. Maybe it wasn't. But just finding new meaning in a letter that you knew you had is wonderful too.

175

Spirits use a lot of synchronicities— or coincidences— which are signs in repetition. This includes things like seeing a sign on a bus, or a license plate with a number that resonates with you, like maybe your loved one's birthday. Or you'll hear something on the radio or on social media over and over and think, "*Wow, I've heard that a lot lately. It must mean something.*"

They also use animals and objects. They'll send you dragonflies, birds, butterflies, feathers, coins, and rainbows.

I've also already talked about orbs, but sometimes you'll see them in different colors that resonate, or you'll see flickers or streaks of light. You might also see shadows and shadow figures.

It's also common to sense a presence. You just know that someone is there.

You might also recognize a loved one in another person. "*That person at the bus stop looked like…*" or people crossing our paths giving us the same message.

Symbols:

Mediumship is not like picking up the phone and having a conversation. You'll use your clairs to receive different symbols. It's up to you, and the person you're reading for, to piece together what the message means. For example, if I see a watch, it could mean someone was given a watch by a loved one, or it could mean that this person's time here was cut short. My symbol for a hard-worker or someone who worked with their hands is a red flannel shirt.

You can ask for Spirit to show you what you need to understand. "*Please show me a dragonfly if you are someone's father.*" Create a symbol dictionary as you start this process. Always ask yourself what a symbol means for you. *Did you begin playing with your hair when you usually don't?* Maybe this person's hair was important to them? *Do you hear coins jingling?* Maybe this person always had change in their pocket or they worked with money. *Do you suddenly have a headache?* Maybe this person died from something head related. Think about what certain colors, animals, uniforms for occupations, holidays, hobbies, or locations mean for you. Anything. Start a journal as you figure it out!

FIVE

◆ ◆ ◆

Water

I Have A Secret

"I've always been an outcast in the spiritual sense. I was raised Mormon, which put me in the "weird" category with my friends growing up. I haven't been to church since I was a kid, and the religion never really spoke to me personally. But most of my family still attends church and practices a Mormon faith. I can't tell you how many times in my life that I've been sitting in a room with people who don't know my family or upbringing, and they start making fun of what Mormons believe, or saying they're awful to women, or that they're a cult...etc. I listen, get really uncomfortable, but smile and nod. I feel like such a freak.

I don't associate with any religion now. I've been to some non-denominational church services, and I learned a lot about Judaism after my dad married my stepmom and we got to know her amazing Jewish family, friends, and traditions. My husband grew up Christian, but organized religion in general never spoke to him either. Our children don't attend church even though we've contemplated it a lot since we feel all religion teaches you morals. ...But I can tell you now that I'm more spiritual and more connected to a higher source (call it God?) than I have ever been, as I learn mediumship and understand how to use my intuition.

So I'm a medium? I don't know yet. You can say I've been "called" to do this. Why would I choose to continue to be labeled "weird" otherwise? I feel like I understand what it was like for my gay friends and family members to come out of the closet. That's what it's like for me. I didn't choose this. It's just who I am. And I'm really afraid of what people will think of me.

Well, the uncomfortable nod and smile happened again. But not with Mormons this time...with psychics. My best friend grew up as a really strict Christian, and she still is. I have "come out" to some of my friends and family as I develop my skills as a medium, healer, and intuitive. But I block her (and a few others) from a lot of posts and I don't tell her what's going on with me because I know that she wouldn't understand. The other day, she started telling me about a TV show she saw where a woman who claimed to be psychic was scamming the families of murder victims out of money saying she could help and was called out on it. I said, "Wow that's really sad. She gives real psychics who do this sort of help for detectives a really bad reputation." And she laughed and said no one could really help with that.

Earlier that same day, we were picking up some pizzas for our kids. She ordered the pizza and came back to the car while we waited for them to bake. We were both watching a young couple with backpacks talking at the edge of the strip mall. The woman grabbed a couple of dollars out of her pocket and went into a sandwich shop and came back with a small cup of soup and two spoons. They sat on the side-walk and shared. My friend said, "Do you think they're homeless or wandering backpackers?" I said I didn't know but they looked clean. She went back inside to pick up our pizzas, and came back out with an extra one and handed them a whole pizza. They were so appreciative and waved and smiled as we pulled away. I said, "Aww that's so sweet you bought them a pizza." And she said, "I was just called to do it for them. God told me to do it."

So when this conversation with the fraud psychic came up later and she was telling me that there was no such thing as someone with real gifts like that... I said, "I really feel that there are people who use their intuition for good and I feel like it comes from God." And she said, "God wouldn't do that." So I said, "Why is it so hard to believe that the same inner voice that told you to buy that couple a pizza, is the same inner voice that some people use to help find a murder victim and comfort a grieving family?" She didn't really have an answer, but we talked a little about false prophets in the bible and how that doesn't have anything to do with gifts people have. (What do I know? I don't read the bible.) I said, "You gave those people a pizza out of good intentions and love. If a medium gives messages out of the same place, then they aren't doing anything wrong." I guess she kind of agreed, but we mostly agreed to disagree.

This friend and I are like two peas in a pod of laughter. We think alike, talk alike, were each other's maid of honor, our kids and husbands are best friends too, and I'd like to think she'd love me no matter what. And like I said before, she knows nothing about the energy medicine and intuitive development classes I've been taking, the books I read, or the amazing messages I've been able to give people this past year or so. She doesn't know that I was talking about myself when I was defending psychics. But I think that she would feel that if I go down this road, I must be working for the devil, and it stops me from telling her anything about it. All I know is that I'm doing all of this out of love and I believe I have more of a higher connection than I ever have before. I used to call her and ask her to pray for my flights before we took off like she had some direct line to God that I didn't have access to. I haven't asked her to do that in months because I have my own faith now. I'm not sure if she's noticed.

In this world, there are good people and bad people. Good energy and bad energy. People who do things for the wrong reasons, and people who do things for the right reasons. There are Mormons who are complete hypocrites and treat their families terribly, and there's my aunt and uncle who treat each other with love and respect, and give tours of the Mormon Conference Center in Salt Lake City and never press the religion on me. There are awful fraud psychics and people who channel lower energies for profit, and people who channel out of love and just want to receive a little financial reimbursement for these gifts, since it takes time away from their families or another better-paying job. It's kind of funny that this just popped into my head since my friend is a huge Disney freak but... from The Little Mermaid... "I don't understand how a world that makes such wonderful things could be bad." This world isn't bad, but there's plenty of bad people in it, which is what Ariel's father is afraid of. He didn't *need to be afraid, and I need to learn to stand with this secret I have.*

-JULY 30, 2016

My journal thoughts one year later:

I sent "I have a secret" to my former best friend. She told me I was doing the devil's work and I was going to hell. We haven't spoken since.

I have changed so much since then. I am a medium. I am a healer. Those who have felt called to see me feel safe while crying their heart out in my studio (or over the phone or by video chat). I offer them comfort, guidance, breakthrough, and closure.

I have learned that what I do has nothing to do with me. I'm a channel, a middle-man, just there to help my clients come in contact with their higher selves, loved ones, and the universe. They heal themselves.

I have absolutely beautiful soul friends now. If I'm going to hell, it's worth it, and I'm going with the most amazing people I know.

Don't live your life in fear of what others think of you. Be you. Shine. Use your gifts. The world needs more love."

Coming Out Of The Broom Closet

I had a lot of work to do to become who I am today. I'm not sure why showing tourists how to use scientific equipment was so much more acceptable than using my own sixth sense. It's as if my tours were a party trick and I was congratulated on duping everyone and making money, but using my own gifts one-on-one with clients makes me a crazy person. It also makes people question my relationship with God, the Universe, the Divine, etc. It becomes religious and biblical when it doesn't need to be. It has been a struggle "coming out of the broom closet" and becoming my true self, and I'm still not all the way there. So if you're feeling the same way, as a healer in hiding, I'm here to tell you that I understand.

I have friends who are deeply religious and most are supportive of what I do and understand that I do this for a much higher purpose. They constantly tell me that I am deeply gifted. It has been a very long spiritual journey for me and no matter how far I go, I still don't quite understand or believe it myself most days.

It's a long, tough road full of doubts and feeling like I'm making everything up. I have feelings of, *"Why me?"* *"Why am I special?"* *"What the hell am I doing?"* But the more people I help connect with their loved ones, the more tissues I hand out, the more I learn and grow about this crazy life we live.

I believe we all came here for a reason. We have a purpose to fulfill. And when we have learned that lesson, we die and go back where we came. We are souls having human experiences. This is where our soul grows. And we either embrace our purpose or we fight it, die, and try again next time. I feel that my purpose here is pretty freaking huge. And I can't wait for the next chapter.

Souldust

Souldust is one of my favorite weekend retreats in the Pacific Northwest and it deserves its own completely seperate chapter. It is an adult summer camp with all sorts of "woo-woo" classes meant for soul work, such as yoga, meditation, intuition, healing, writing, astrology, and even relaxing sound baths. There are also typical camp activities such as archery, hiking, canoeing, and even a climbing wall. It's held in the mossy damp green forest of the Key Peninsula, and it is pure magic.

My first year attending was spent as a Camp Counselor. I chose my cabin mascot as the Black Cats, and my cabin-mates were all amazing witchy women with a cool dark vibe and a love of the supernatural. Rachel, Souldust's founder, used a pendulum to decide which cabin each camper would belong, much like The Sorting Hat in Harry Potter. It was uncanny where everyone ended up, and were completely meant to be. We became family that weekend.

I also spent that first year offering private sessions, just as I did in my studio at my home. "Spirit Spa Sessions" were my most popular service, and it was perfect to be able to offer them at Souldust. My Spirit Spa Session was a transformational, intuitive healing meant to help guide you on your soul's journey while leaving you feeling relaxed, renewed, and balanced. The unique experience included reiki, sound healing, massage, gentle touch of acupressure points, essential oils, and meta-physical tools such as stones, crystals, sage, palo santo, sea salt, and a pendulum. The session flowed like water, touching upon chakra points from head to toe. You would breathe and journey in a meditative and grounded state. During the session, I was open to receiving spirit messages that I would jot down and discuss after the hands-on portion, as well as pulling tarot cards if more clarity was needed. My Spirit Spa Session left my clients feeling uplifted, light, and touched by Spirit.

I mean, that sounds freaking amazing, right?! I was booked solid. I was the only practitioner who was sold out before camp even started. I ended up experiencing a lot of deep soul work myself during that first camp. I realized that I felt unworthy, and even guilty, for having the most popular session when there were so many amazing teachers and practitioners attending. I doubted my own gifts and sometimes felt that the messages I was receiving were maybe a fluke or even simply just luck. I didn't trust myself to give messages to these magical humans who were eagerly expecting. But I learned—and still learn, again and again— that it wasn't about me. It never is. I learned to get out of my own way, just relax, and just be. And of course each client who saw me that weekend had a life changing, wonderful experience.

Through workshops and journaling that weekend, I learned to be grateful. I was filled with gratitude, but also very humble. I was grateful to be there and to be able to offer my gifts. I was grateful for a full schedule and grateful for money. I was grateful to become part of such an amazing community of healers, and to remember how to give and how to receive. I learned more and more about how to be myself, and to stop trying so hard to control outcomes.

In the weeks leading up to camp, I had offered to teach a class about mediumship and ghost hunting. I was politely turned down, and was told there were already enough workshops to

fill the weekend. But with my newfound confidence and gratitude, my new community of best witch friends told me I should
"go rogue" and do a ghost hunt late one night after all the
workshops were finished for the evening. Of course I brought
my ghost hunting gear— thinking maybe I'd do an informal fun
ghost hunt one evening for my Black Cats. However, so many
campers heard about my equipment, that they wanted to see
how it all worked. Fortunately I had access to another cabin
up the path a little way from my Black Cat cabin to use for my
private sessions. I tucked my massage table in a corner and laid
out my ghost hunting equipment on a table in the middle of the
room, surrounded by bunk beds. It was going to be like a fun
childhood camp ghost story night.

My Black Cats and I made post-it notes with the time and cabin
name to stick all over camp. *"Ghost Hunt Tonight. 10:30pm
Sleem Cabin,"* they said. I even got up the nerve to stand up in
front of everyone at the evening campfire to announce our little
get-together, promising it isn't as scary as everyone seemed to
think it might be. Close to twenty campers arrived that evening. They arranged themselves on the bunk beds, spreading out
on top and bottom bunks for the best view. I went into my usual
spiel— ingrained in my brain from my days in Salem about how
the equipment worked— and told them a bit about myself and
my experience. A few campers were visibly apprehensive to be
in this dark cabin in the middle of the woods with a ouija board
on the table. I explained that it has always been my mission to
take the fear out of the unknown, and we began our investigation, just like old times.

There wasn't any ghostly activity, but I really felt there were
some family members there in spirit. I suggested trying a new
way to use a spirit box. I told them that a spirit box scans radio
signals quickly, and spirits can use radio frequency to chime in
with a word here and there. However, it was always a difficult
piece of equipment to use for first-timers, as it's hard to not con-
fuse the short sound of a song on a radio or a DJ, and a true para-

normal voice. So I decided to try using it in a completely new way:

I put on my noise-cancelling headphones and turned the spirit box up so that I could no longer hear conversations in the room. I would listen intently, and speak any word that I heard, while I nominated a friend to ask questions to the spirits who might be there. I thought it might result in a bunch of random words that made no sense with the questions being asked, but it would be a really fun experiment anyway. So, I went under—so to speak — and put on my headphones. It was actually more eerie than I was expecting to watch barely-lit wide-eyed faces staring at me in the dim light— and hearing nothing but staggered, jerky white noise. I closed my eyes and repeated any word I heard so as to not be influenced by reading the lips of the camper asking the questions. Once in a while, I'd open my eyes, pull one side off my ear, and ask if anything was coming up for anyone since I was pretty much out of the loop. I received enthusiastic comments of *"Yes! Keep going!"* I continued for what felt like forever, as it really was a strange sensory experience under those headphones. Finally, I couldn't do it anymore. My ears and mind started feeling like they were playing tricks on me. I removed the headphones and re-joined the group. I had to be filled in on the messages they were receiving. Turns out, questions were matched up with answers, and beautiful bits and pieces of messages were given while tears were shed. The next day, everyone was talking about the amazing experience they shared the night before, so naturally, at the next camp, I was invited to teach a similar evening as a scheduled workshop.

My workshop was called, "A Spirited Evening Campfire" and was advertised online as, *"Stick around after the all-camp campfire for "ghost stories" that are actually beautiful signs from our loved ones who have passed. This fireside workshop focuses on taking the fear out of the unknown and using our own intuition to connect with the other side. After sharing our stories of spirit, the night will include an explanation of spirit energy, communication, debunking, intui-*

tive exercises, signs and symbols, and protection from spirits who are not welcome. You'll then sit quietly as Kim uses her tools of the trade— from ghost hunting equipment such as EMF detectors and audio recorders— to metaphysical tools such as pendulums, dowsing rods, and tarot cards— and our own intuition! Loved ones on the other side often use the evening as an opportunity to come through so participants may receive an impromptu mediumship reading as well."

Phew. That was a mouthful, but campers were really excited about attending. So excited, in fact, that I was asked to extend my attendee count. My original thought was to keep the event intimate, but 54 people signed up, and even more planned to attend without registering if I gave permission. Ok. The more the merrier? All those years watching *Crossing over with John Edward* as a child, and suddenly I had become him... and that thought was slightly terrifying to me. I realized that everyone was most excited about the prospect of receiving a message, and I didn't want to disappoint. There I went again with the huge doubts in my mind about my gifts. Also, I had the same guilty thoughts as the previous year, as I was competing in the same time slot for an amazing workshop by a couple that I really admire.

That afternoon, I spent a quiet couple of hours on the balcony of the Sleem cabin, overlooking the lake through the evergreen trees. I meditated, and then rewrote my notes for the evening— speaking more about mediumship than paranormal equipment — since that's what this crowd would love to hear about most. As I was writing, I received a really encouraging text from my friend Keao, who is an amazing medium who studies regularly with James Van Praagh. She encouraged and supported me so much the past year to stop being a "healer in hiding". Hearing from her a couple hours before the workshop really helped calm the nerves. I was reminded again to get out of my own way.

The rest of the afternoon and evening, I felt completely guided and ready. After the evening campfire, I set up my equipment on the small stage-like platform and sat on the edge while I waited for campers to file back in on the bleachers with fresh cups of cocoa or coffee. The fire warmed us all in the cool spring air as we told stories of loved ones in spirit. I spoke quickly about my background and my equipment, and I told my eager audience that I knew that what they were here for was a message from someone close on the other side. I left my equipment sitting on the stage, faced my audience, and began to center myself. I closed my eyes, took a few deep breaths, and started getting all sorts of tiny snippets of information. Names, feelings, songs, and more. And I couldn't really narrow in on who the messages were for. This was the most people I've ever had for a group reading. I've done a few in my home studio, but for very intimate groups. This felt like a whole bunch of people all trying to push in line and yell their message first. I attempted to relay a few, but they were choppy and only small bits made sense to someone at a time. I felt like I was jumping all over the place. Suddenly I had the idea to use my spirit box again... although I knew this time was going to be very different.

I explained to the crowd that extra centering might be needed this evening, reminded them about the use of a spirit box, and put on my headphones. I heard a few short words, took off my headphones, and repeated them. It was then that I was able to narrow in on whom the message was for, and to receive and give the message for one person at a time. I did this for almost two hours. State a few words, someone resonated with them, and I would finish the message without my headphones, filling in the rest of the message with my "clairs,"— particularly what I saw, heard, and felt. These campers received amazing messages from spirit that night, and I was reminded once again that there's no reason to be afraid.

Meeting My Future Self

"I was sailing down a river to meet my future self and see my future home. The wind died down, and my small sailboat came to a stop at a huge home that almost looked like a castle. I saw stone walls and a beautiful red front door with wrought iron accents. I got out of my boat, walked to the door, and knocked. The door opened to reveal a fit, thin, wealthy-looking woman. This woman did not feel like me. Sailing on a river felt like me. She smiled and invited me to come inside. Everything was ornate and beautiful, although very expensive. It felt unusable. Everything looked very stiff and uncomfortable, and I did not sit even though this woman was friendly. She handed me a small round box. Maybe a music box, or a mirror, or some sort of antique trinket box, I wasn't sure. I thanked her and climbed back into my sailboat to continue on my journey.

What was this box? I researched trinket boxes in the Victorian era. They were meant to keep curiosities, souvenirs, gadgets, and knickknacks. What did I need this for? I described the box that I saw to my husband and he said matter-of-factly, "It's a compass."

When we were living in Salem, he had a necklace custom made for me of a silver seven-pointed star with a blue sapphire set in the middle to match my wedding ring. He wanted me to have a star that was uniquely mine and would help me find my way.

Now we embark on our greatest journey to faraway lands and exotic cultures, the sea as our road, and the stars of the Universe and the electromagnetic field of Earth's energy guiding us and leading the

Kimberly Bizjak

way."

-MAY 30, 2017

Changing Tides

I had a dream that I was standing at my bedroom window staring out at the calm ocean. The ocean became choppy with tight little rocking waves. Those waves became larger and more spread out, and soon the entire shoreline became bare and dry as the water retreated completely. And then huge white waves would crash back into the land. These rolling waves became bigger and violent as they swallowed the homes on the hill below my house. I stood there in wonder but I wasn't afraid. I watched the waves reach my window with a thundering sound as it crashed against the glass. And, as suddenly as the sea came, I watched through the salt it left behind on the window as it slowly returned back to its glassy smooth surface in the distance.

I'm an Intuitive Medium. Because I work between life and death everyday, I truly understand how short life is. We're born, we work to live and live to work, and then we die. My sessions help my clients find their true path in this life with the help of their loved ones on the other side.

Having no regrets is a huge theme in my sessions.

Considering that I spend my time helping people reach their higher purpose, this year I decided that it's time to take my own advice and do the same.

I'm in the process of starting fresh and beginning a new life with my husband and two young kids. As I write this, we're in the process of selling everything we own to move onto a sailboat and circumnavigate the world.

My husband and I have always loved to sail. Being out on the open water always feels so freeing, and my absolute favorite part of sailing is that moment when— after motoring out of the marina and it's hectic and chaotic trying to pull the sails up and they're flapping around in the wind and the sound of the motor is vibrating into your brain— you cut the engine.

Silence.

You hear every crinkle of the sails and the water splashing against the boat as you slice through it, you smell the salty air, the sunshine, the wind. There, in the quiet that exists only when you remove every artificial noise possible, it's just you; and the power of Mother Nature.

As I heed my own advice, I'm reminded of how important it is to our intuition to feel this force of nature that's bigger than ourselves. It's exactly like being out at sea, adrift and able to feel the wind shifting on your skin and simply knowing which direction you're heading next. That knowing allows us to adjust our sails appropriately; you feel where you're meant to go.

If you just listened, you'll end up exactly where you are meant to be.

So I listened. *We* listened, and we decided to let go, to turn off the motor. We're letting go of the concept of the "normal life" we're "supposed" to live, and we are letting go of all the things that society says we should own.

Sometimes it feels liberating.

Sometimes it feels absolutely terrifying.

I have fears. Fear of the unknown, fear of not succeeding, fear of not having money to sustain our nomadic lifestyle, fear of what people think of us, fear of failure, and especially fear that we are going to "screw up" our children.

But then we think about how amazing this unusual life will be for them.

We want our kids to be citizens of the world, and by changing our lives this way, we're giving them that. We also want to connect and grow closer, and we're excited to be spending real time as a family every single day as we sail, to really know each other in a way we never would living on land. Connect with each other as we connect with the sea. And, yes, we can't predict that everything will turn out the way we plan, or hope, or that we'll be able to avoid our fears coming true. But that's part of the power of this move—— it's one based in trust. It's putting faith in ourselves. It's the decision to change our sails because the wind of our souls changed direction.

It's our choice now to go with the flow and not fight it.

To have no regrets of unsailed seas.

To find our home amid those glassy, choppy, uncertain waters.

-DECEMBER 2017

About The Author

Kimberly Bizjak is a Holistic Therapist & Intuitive Medium, currently sailing the world with her husband and two kids. (And her cat!)

As a digital nomad, Kim sees clients through video chat and email who are feeling "stuck" in their own spiritual journey. She clears energetic blocks through the use of tarot, chakra healing, astrology, meditation, mediumship, and more.

Known as a Personal Navigator from the sea, her mission is to "Take the fear out of the unknown" by helping people embrace change, and believe in the impossible.

Visit her website at www.seeingfromthesea.com
and follow her family's adventures at
www.lifeoffthedeepend.com

12863373R00116

Made in the USA
Monee, IL
30 September 2019